OUT OF THE
SHADOWS

Out of The Shadows
Copyright© 2019 by Theresa Sederholt

ISBN: 978-1-7343894-0-1

The author acknowledges the copyrighted or trademarked status and trademark owners of the following wordmarks mentions in this work of fiction: iPad, Child Protective Services, McDonalds, Fortnite, Call of Duty, Madden NFL, Harry Potter and The Chamber of Secrets, Nissan Versa, Farina, Shake Shack.

This is a work of fiction. Names, characters, businesses, places, events, and incidents are either the products of the author's imagination or used in a fictitious manner. Any resemblance to actual persons, living or dead, or actual events is purely coincidental.

This book contains strong language, and violence. It is not intended for anyone under the age of 18. Warning: this book may contain triggers for victims of domestic violence.

Publisher: Theresa Sederholt©
Author: Theresa Sederholt
Cover designer/formatter: Stacey Blake, Champagne Book Design
Editor: Jacquelyn Ayres
Photographer: Dante Dellamore
Model: Robert Kelly

Special thank you to, Master Technician Scott Detwiler.
Your knowledge and help was invaluable.

"I learned that courage was not the absence of fear, but the triumph over it. The brave man is not he who does not feel afraid, but he who conquers that fear." —*Nelson Mandela*

OUT OF THE SHADOWS

CHAPTER ONE

Brady

DAD, PLEASE STOP CRYING. *I* TRIED SO HARD TO *stop her . . . to protect you, Dad, to protect us. I didn't want to hurt her, but it was the only way* I could save you—save us. I had to stop her. I'm so sorry, Daddy. Hello? Why won't you answer me? Are you mad at me? I look around, and everyone in the room is going about their business. Why is everyone acting like I'm not here? *Hello, can you hear me? Can anyone hear me?* I don't understand; why can't anyone hear me? I try to yell really loud so everyone can hear, but nothing comes out. I have no voice left. I'm sitting in the chair across from my dad, but he doesn't look up at me. He's is crying uncontrollably. I've never seen my dad cry before. He wipes his eyes as he talks to the person in the bed. It must be my mom, but how could that be? I stabbed her while she was beating

Daddy. She has to be dead. People usually die when they get stabbed. When I lean in to get a closer look, I gasp. It's me! How could that be me? How could I be in two places at the same time? For the first time in my life, I'm really scared. *Daddy, please look up at me. I'm here and I'm okay. She didn't hurt me like she said she would. Nothing. Why am I'm being kept silent, left on the sidelines, watching and listening?*

The door opens and a woman comes in. She goes to the bed and touches me. I watch as my body jerks. Not all women are bad like my mom, yet I can't help being afraid of her touch. Daddy jumps up and squeezes my hand.

"He moved. That's a good sign, right?"

"It's normal for someone under heavy sedation to have spontaneous movements. We will try to keep him heavily sedated so we can give the swelling around his brain a chance to subside. I assure you, Mr. Johnson, we are doing everything possible to help your son. Now that we have him settled in, why don't you let one of the doctors tend to your injuries?" She sounds nice and she wants to help us. He doesn't answer her, only shaking his head no. That's when I notice the blood on the side of his head. I thought I stopped her, but she still hurt him. "The police are outside the room and want to speak with you."

"I'm not leaving my son's side. If they want to talk, let them in. As far as my injuries are concerned, I've survived a lot worse."

She steps away from the bed. "As you wish, but if you get lightheaded or your headache becomes worse, please let one of us help you." She opens the door to leave and two men in suits come in. I've watched enough television shows to know they must be the cops that the lady was talking about.

"Mr. Johnson, I know this is not a good time, but we need to ask you some questions while the events are still fresh in your mind."

"My son is in a coma, and my wife put him here. What else do you need to know?"

"We need to know the events leading up to this. What would make her do this to the boy?"

"Is she dead?"

His voice is low and it's hard for me to hear. I lean in closer; I don't want to miss anything. "She's in surgery now. Why don't you tell me what happened."

"I came home from work and she was beating Brady. I grabbed the first thing I could, which was a knife and stabbed her. I called 911, but they were taking too long. I put Brady in my car and raced here to the emergency room. He's an innocent boy, caught in the middle of my nightmare."

Dad, Dad, please stop lying. I did it—not you. When I came in and yelled for her to stop, she wouldn't. It's only after I stabbed her that she turned the bat on me. Tell them the truth Dad; she was beating you again. She said she would kill me in front of you, and I couldn't take it anymore. I grabbed the knife and stuck it in her, not you. I'm trying to yell but nothing is coming out.

"With all due respect, sir, your story doesn't fit what we found at the scene. Now, do you want to change your story and tell us what really happened?"

"Lawyer, I want my lawyer. Until that time, I have nothing to say to you. Now, leave my son and me alone. We've been through enough."

3

The officer places a card on the bed next to Dad and they leave. Why is he covering for me? Why?

Dane

Life changes. Sometimes for the good. But for me, it was the worse. How has my life spun so far out of control? I close my eyes and try to make sense of it all.

I met Julie my senior year of high school. To say I fell hard and fast is an understatement. She was on the varsity softball team. I was captain of the wrestling team. A match made in heaven, or so I thought. What I realized afterwards—it was hormones that were unleashed that day, not a match made in heaven.

After graduation, I made the decision to join the Navy. My lifelong dream was to be a SEAL. I knew I couldn't let anyone or anything get in the way of that. When I broke the news to Julie, she freaked out. That right there should have been a sign, you know . . . a red flag. However, I was a cocky kid and, bless her heart, she did everything she could to try and talk me out of it. I rub my temples, remembering that day like it was yesterday.

"Dane, you can't leave me and your parents. There's so much here for you, for us. Why would you throw it all away?"

"This has always been my dream, Julie, you knew that. We can still be together. Go to college but wait for me. I promise, I'll come back."

"I can't guarantee I'm going to be here when you get back. I can't put my life on hold for empty promises."

That should have been another sign, but again, I was too green, young, and stupid. She was my first girlfriend. So, I did the only thing I could think of; I asked her to marry me. With one condition, we do it after I finish basic training. She agreed, or at least I thought she did. You see, at that age, I took everything at face value. Now, of course, I know better. Fast forward to two days before I was supposed to leave for basic training and that's when she dropped the bombshell on me.

"Dane, I'm pregnant."

"What do you mean, pregnant? You said you were on the pill!"

"It's not 100 percent, nothing ever is. I want to get married before you leave." When I look back on this now, all the pieces to the puzzle were so clear to everyone but me. She played me like a fool. My parents saw through her games and they tried to talk me out of it. I ignored their warnings. After all, I was eighteen and I thought I had all the answers.

"Why do we have to rush? Let me get through my training. You can plan everything and when I get back, we can get married."

"Oh, no. What if something happens to you? I'll be stuck with this baby and all the expenses on my own. At least, if we get married right now, the baby and I will be covered."

Stuck? Another set of alarm bells should have been going off, but again, I was young and in love, or at least I thought so.

5

"Are you expecting me to die or something?"

"Of course not. I love you and I want to make sure that our baby is protected. That's what a good mother does, Dane. Besides, your pay will be more if you are married. We can save that for the baby."

"What about you going away to college?"

"I'll go to the local community college. Don't worry; it will all work out."

She had an answer for everything, and, at the time, it all made sense. My parents didn't believe she was really pregnant; they urged me again to wait. Reluctantly, I went along with Julie. We got married and the next day I shipped out. During training I had to block out everything, including Julie. After my twenty-four-week Basic Underwater Demolition Seal camp, I received a letter saying I passed. While I was waiting for a spot to open for the twenty-eight-week extensive qualification training camp, I was shipped out to Naval Station Rota in Spain. I was there for three years, waiting for my chance to prove myself at Seal camp. I asked Julie to join me in Spain, but she refused. Her first excuse was she wanted the baby to be born in the States. Soon enough, Julie gave birth to Brady. I wasn't there, and she never let me live that down. After that, every time I asked, it was one excuse after another.

When a spot opened up in camp, I was given a two-week leave to go home and tie up any loose ends. When I got home, I found a very bitter person. But at least I had my son. I vowed right then and there that I would dedicate my life to him.

I knew that my time at the qualification camp was the make it or break it for the SEALS. I was always a gym rat, so I had no problem with the physical stuff. However, I had to block out everyone and everything so I could keep my head in the game to try and grab my dream. In the end, nine members of my class made it and I wasn't one of them. As much as I didn't want my personal life to affect me, it ended up making me a weak link. After that, I did an eight-year stint in the Navy, but I never made it my career; my heart just wasn't in it. By the time I left the Navy, my parents had passed, and I completed my degree in IT. Julie, on the other hand, never completed her degree. Just another thing she blamed me for and, ultimately, Brady, too.

CHAPTER TWO

THE BEEPING OF THE MACHINES IS IN RHYTHM with my heart. As long as they keep going, so will I. I've been able to protect Brady, at least up until today. Julie used him as leverage over me, and I let her. Growing up, my parents taught me to never hit a woman. I was told to always show manners and respect, so how should I defend myself? How do I protect my son? I'm glad my parents are not alive today to see what's become of me.

Leaving was never an option. I could fight her for custody but who would believe me? I wouldn't leave Brady behind to deal with her on his own. I tried to seek help once; I found an online support group. Since I live in a small Ohio town, I thought this was a good idea, a way to keep my anonymity. Unfortunately, they were of no help to me. Oh, sure they gave me the typical advice. Leave, if possible, never retaliate, and get evidence of the abuse. Get a restraining order and an order of protection for my son. All good advice, just not for my situation. I did look into some shelters, but I couldn't find any that would help a man with a small child. Some people even came up with crazy ideas on how I should get rid of her. It's amazing what people will say when they hide behind a keyboard. All this did was to reaffirm what I already knew. There is a stigma surrounding domestic violence when it comes to the man. Society has no clue how to deal with it and, honestly, neither do I. After that, I found out that mental abuse was just as bad as physical abuse. When Julie couldn't take her abuse on me physically, she would resort to mental abuse. I wanted to walk away . . . so many times. Once, I tried to do just that. Unfortunately, that's when she started to use Brady as a weapon against me. That's when the physical abuse got worse for me.

One day, I decided to offer her an out. I figured she had to be miserable, so why not? I told her I would give her a divorce. I offered her money, the house—anything she wanted. All I asked for was full custody of Brady. I would even give her unlimited supervised visitation. She laughed and vowed to never let me walk away with my son. That was the day I saw how evil she really was.

I kept trying to come up with some sort of solution, you know, a plan. Most people would have given up but I'm not most people. I decided to offer to pay for her tuition. I thought if she got her degree, she would find her purpose in life. After all, everyone needs a purpose. All that earned me was a coffee mug thrown at my head.

With no degree or any kind of training, Julie went to

work in retail. She picked up as many shifts as she could, probably to get away from us. One night after work, she went out for drinks with her friends. She had her friends and I had mine. They never mingled. The only one I've ever met was Janelle. She is everything opposite of Julie: Janelle has very short bleach-blonde hair and is a large lady whereas Julie has very long black hair and is very fit.

By the time Julie came home, she was drunk… to the point of passing out. I was at the point in my life where I really didn't care what she did, except she drove herself home. One night I sat up in the living room, watching her stumble through the front door.

"What would possess you to get behind the wheel of a car in the condition you're in?!"

"What the fuck do you care?" Her words so slurred, they were barely audible.

"I care about who you could have killed. I care about my son and the repercussions this could have on him. Did you ever think what he would have to deal with if his mother was con-victed of vehicular manslaughter?" Totally disgusted, I got up and head toward the bedroom. As I passed her, she grabbed an umbrella out of the stand. I heard a swooshing sound before I saw the handle making contact with the side of my face. I had no time to react. I guess I was in shock. I never expected her to hit me in the face. It was always a punch in the arm, a shove, or a flying coffee cup. I wrote it off as the effects of too much alcohol as I headed to bed. Without a doubt, I had a lump on my face the next morning.

After the umbrella incident, things seemed to quiet down. I thought maybe it was just a one-time thing, you know, frustration mixed with alcohol. I was so wrong.

That was the start of hell for my son and me. I took the beatings because if I would attempt to do anything about it, she would threaten to beat Brady and blame me. Who do you think the authorities would believe? Brady was too young to understand what was happening, or at least I thought so, so I took it. As long as she didn't drink, I was able to keep the situation under control—almost normal, whatever that is.

As time went on, Brady found ways to keep himself busy. He got involved with sports, which gave Julie more time for herself. I hoped she would find an outlet for her frustrations, something other than me. Since my being around seemed to bring out the worst in her. I went to the gym two hours before work. Then I worked long days to keep my distance. I made sure I came home for dinner every night and spent my evenings with my son. Looking back now, I realize what I thought was helping was only hurting her more. When Brady turned thirteen, everything came to a head.

I was in my office when my assistant buzzed me that Brady's school was on the line. They never call me, only Julie. I quickly grabbed the phone, "*This is Dane; is my son okay?*"

"*Mr. Johnson, this is Abigail Scott, Brady's guidance counselor. I happened to be working the carpool line today. Mrs. Johnson came to pick him up and she was not acting right. I didn't feel comfortable letting him go home with her.*

I held him back and had him go to my office while she caused a scene."

"What do you mean 'she wasn't acting right?'" I held my breath, anticipating the worst.

"Mr. Johnson, I believe she was drunk. When I asked her about it, she let loose with a string of language that was very inappropriate. I tried to stop her from speeding off but there wasn't much I could do. I'm sure she will file a formal complaint with the superintendent, which might end up costing me my job. However, I couldn't in good conscious let Brady get in the car with her."

"Is Brady still with you?"

"Yes, I can stay here until you come and get him. But I think we need to talk about what's going on at home."

"I'm on my way." I hung up, grabbed my keys and headed out. Thankfully, I was only fifteen minutes from the school. Julie knows how I feel about drinking and driving. What would possess her to go pick up Brady while she was shitfaced? When I pulled up, the lot was almost empty. I signed in at the front desk and headed over to get Brady. I found him with Ms. Scott, doing his homework. When he saw me coming in, his bottom lip began to quiver. The boy was thirteen years old and shouldn't have been fighting back tears. He should've been outside exploring the world.

"Hey, buddy." I quickly pulled him into a hug.

"I'm sorry, Dad."

When I pulled back, I noticed a tear that he quickly wiped away.

"None of this is your fault, Brady, and you have nothing to be sorry for. I'm going to step outside with Ms. Scott; you continue working on your homework."

When we stepped into the hallway, I took a deep breath and tried to compose myself. *"Ms. Scott, I'm sorry you were put in this position. I will talk to the superintendent on your behalf,"* I told her.

"It's Abby, and that won't be necessary. A couple of other teachers where there and they already documented everything. My concern is Brady. I haven't called in Child Protective Services yet; I wanted to talk to you first. Please don't take offence to this but I have to ask. Is he safe at home?"

The knot in my stomach got tighter. *"Please don't call CPS. I can assure you he is safe. I will make other arrangements for his transportation to and from school."* She looked at me, for what . . . I don't know.

"I'm sorry, but I'm required by law to call them. Besides, it's in Brady's best interest."

I wondered—do I tell this woman what's been going on? Will she be able to help me, or will I be putting myself in a worse position than I am now? *"You call whomever you have to, right now I need to get Brady home."* is how I answered.

She reached into her pocket, pulled out a pen and sticky note pad. I watched as she jotted down a number. I was sure it was for some sort of agency that she thought would help us.

"This is my cell number; you don't need to go through this alone." She pressed the paper into my hand. I wondered if she had any clue as to what I was going through? Before I could say anything, she opened her office door and headed inside. I helped Brady gather his stuff and we left. I made sure to put Ms. Scott's number in my pocket.

"Dad, is everything okay?" Brady looked up at me.

I pulled him close. *"Yeah, everything is fine. How about we go to McDonald's for an early dinner."* It's his favorite and I was sure it would cheer him up.

"What about mom?" he inquired. As he reached for the car handle, I notice his hand is shaking for the first time. *What the fuck am I doing?* I thought. *I've got to get help; I've got to get someone to believe me.* *"Let's just do a guy's night out tonight."* He didn't need to know that his mom was probably at home passed out by then.

We were early for the dinner rush and, thankfully, the place was pretty empty. After we ordered more food than I knew we could eat, Brady got all the condiments and took a seat at a table in the corner while I waited for everything. I knew I couldn't let the situation with Julie go on any longer, I just didn't have a clue as to where to begin. The only thing I knew for sure was that I had to keep my son safe.

The food showed up pretty quickly. Brady must have seen the three trays and ran over to help. We sat in silence, not sure if it was my inability on where to start or the carb and fat overload we were experiencing. I finally pulled my head out of my ass and broached the subject of what happened that day.

"How many times has your mom shown up at school like she did today?" He was swirling his fry in his ranch dressing, avoiding any eye contact. This told me it had happened before.

"Dad, she was never as bad as she was today."

"Brady, you're not in trouble, at all. However, I don't ever want you getting into the car with her when she's like that. I might not be able to control what she does, but I'm responsible for you. I need you to promise me you will never get in the car with her when she's like that."

"Well, what am I supposed to do; she's my mom, and I have to listen to her, don't I?"

This is where it always gets tough. "Yes and no. When your safety is at stake then, it's a hard no. I won't lie to you or hide stuff from you." I took a long, slow breath, trying to steady my nerves. "Your mom has a drinking problem. I can't stop her from getting behind the wheel, but I can stop you from getting in the car with her." I watched his eyes, trying to gauge his reaction. He squinted and wrinkled his forehead. It's something he's always done when he's confused. I always tease him that his face will get stuck if he keeps doing it. I'm kind of glad that he hasn't stopped to this day; at least I know what his reaction is without asking.

"But what was I supposed to do?"

"At school today, you should have gone up to Ms. Scott or whomever is running the carpool pick-up. If you are at your friend's house, you tell his mom or dad." I reached across the table and dunked one of my fries into his ranch dressing. "I'm also going to get you a new phone. One that does more than just making phone calls. I want you to be able to call me anytime you find yourself in a situation like you were in today, and I want to be able to track you if I need to. You know none of this is your fault, right?" I asked. He gave up on his fries, pushing them away.

"Dad, it's embarrassing when she shows up like she did

today. *My friends are going to make fun of me tomorrow. On top of that, now I have to be tracked?! When does it end?"*

My stomach knotted, knowing how mean kids can be. I knew he was going to have to face a raft of shit, but I wasn't sure how to handle any of this, let alone tell him how to. *"Look, buddy, we are in the same boat. I'm not sure what to do. I promise I will try to figure things out for us, but for the time being, just hold your head up high and ignore the idiots,"* I advised. He piled all our trash onto the tray, got up, and tossed it away. He is the type of boy—when he's done, he's done. I grabbed his backpack and followed quickly behind him out to the car.

"Let's go get your phone before we head home." Most kids would be excited to have a new phone, but Brady just shrugged his shoulders and climbed into the car. Probably knowing why he needed a better phone took away any excitement about getting it.

We weren't in the phone store too long. Not that it would matter; I was sure Julie was out for the count. The ride home was quiet while Brady messed around with the phone. I didn't want Julie to know he had it. I pulled over a block from the house to somehow explain to him why. *"Hey, Brady, I want you to keep the fact that you have a new phone just between us. Do you think you can do that?"* My jaw clenched at the thought of asking my kid to lie. All this because I was at a loss as to how to get out of this big cluster fuck, I'm in.

"*Sure, I doubt she'll even notice, since it looks similar to my old one.*" His voice trailed off and he went back to his phone. I was left wondering what my next move should be or if I even had one.

CHAPTER THREE

B Y THE TIME WE GOT HOME, AS EXPECTED, JULIE
was passed out. I stood in the doorway looking at
her, wondering when did everything go so wrong?
How do I get us safely out of this mess? I pulled the paper
from my pocket with Abby's number. *Do I take a chance
and trust her? Will she think I'm weak? How did I get myself
into this mess and how the fuck do I get out?* I never cared
about myself, only Brady. He's my world and I needed him
safe. I shoved the number back into my pocket. After ten
minutes or so I checked on Brady. I found him fast asleep,
still in his clothes. He finally looked so peaceful; I didn't
have the heart to wake him. I quietly closed his door and
went into the kitchen. The sink was littered with dishes
and trash was everywhere. *How difficult is it to keep this
place clean when no one is hardly ever home?* Brady was
usually at baseball practice and I was working. As I went

about cleaning up the mess, Abby's number was practically burning a hole in my pocket. *Maybe she really can help.* I finished up and grabbed a cup of coffee as I headed out on to the back porch. When I pulled out the number, I quickly looked around. *When did I become so paranoid?* Who the hell was going to see or hear me? My son was fast asleep, and my wife was passed out drunk. I dialed the number but stopped at the last digit, my finger hovering over it. One number away from what—help or a disaster? I finally hit it and she answered on the first ring. *"Hello, Abby, it's Dane, Brady's dad."* Like how many Danes did she know that I had to explain who I was?

"Hi, are you okay? Is Brady okay?"

"Yeah, he's asleep now. I hope it's not too late for you." I realized at that moment that I never even checked the time.

"It's fine. I usually work for at least three hours a night on paperwork. You know a guidance counselor's life is never really over when the school bell rings."

"Abby, did you call CPS?"

"Right to the point, Dane, yes. I really had no choice. They will start an investigation. It's in Brady's best interest."

"Just because you think it's in his best interest, doesn't mean it will keep him safe! What the hell am I supposed to do now?" I tried to hold back my anger, but I wasn't having much luck.

"Dane, what's really going on?"

Do I tell her everything or just what I think will keep CPS away?

"Hello, Dane, are you still there? I'm not the enemy. I want to help, and you have to trust someone."

"I'm in a physically and mentally abusive marriage. Up to this point, I've kept Brady safe. I have offered Julie everything to go away. Well, everything except Brady, but that only made matters worse. She dangles him like a carrot on a stick. She knows I will do anything to protect my son. I'm not sure what to do next. I know I should leave, but not without my son. I have no place to go, and who would believe me?"

"I believe you, Dane. Have you spoken to a lawyer yet?"

"No. I did try a support group but that was a bust. I have no family to turn to for help. I have a couple of friends that I was in the Navy with but I'm not comfortable going to them with my troubles."

"First and foremost, you need a lawyer. Do you have one that you are comfortable with?"

"No. We used Julie's family lawyer when we did our wills."

"If you want, my brother practices family law. He is in the next town over. He's handled this type of situation before. He handled it for me."

I let her words sink in. We were both very quiet. Finally, I found my voice. "I'm sorry; I didn't know. If this brings up too many memories for you, I would totally understand you walking away. The last thing I want is to disrupt your life."

"Thank you, but I'm stronger today than I've ever been before. I will text you Josh's number. I'll also call and let him know you will be getting in touch with him. He can work around your schedule as long as he's not in court."

"What about CPS?"

"I really had no choice; there were a lot of other teachers around. If I didn't report it, someone else would have. I'll let Josh know about the report and he will be able to help you with *that, too. Dane, I just want to say that calling me tonight was a big step. I promise you there is a light at the end of the tunnel. I'm living proof of that. I'm going to hang up now and call him before it gets any later. Get some rest."*

"*Thank you, Abby, for everything.*" She hung up and a few seconds later, my phone chimed with Josh's number. I decided I'd wait until morning to call. I remember finally feeling a sense of hope that night.

CHAPTER FOUR

Brady
One week earlier . . .

I'M UP BEFORE MY ALARM, NOT THAT I GOT MUCH sleep last night. What a clusterfuck of a day. My mom shows up drunk at my school. My guidance counselor calls my dad, and I didn't even get to tell my dad about Danni asking me to the Sadie Hawkins dance. I said yes but I about crapped my pants after she left. Dad was too busy on the phone this morning for me to tell him about it. Mom wasn't even awake yet when we left the house.

When I get to my locker, Danni is waiting for me. See, this right here is my problem—we are best friends. We dump *everything* on each other. So, to say her asking me to the dance was a shocker is an understatement. This now changes our whole friendship! My steps are slow and as I approach, the knot in my stomach gets tighter.

"Hey, you're here early." I try not to look at her and focus on my combination lock instead.

"I wanted to make sure you were okay."

My grip on the dial gets tighter as I rotate it around to the next number. "Does the entire school know?"

"Probably. You know the way things get blown out of proportion here. Look, Brady, I know it's a fucked-up situation but just ignore it. If you keep bringing attention to it, so will everyone else. It's not like you can change anything at this point."

She is the only one I've shared everything with. The fact that my mom is a drunk and beats up on my dad. How, when he's not around, I've caught a few beatings of my own. I quickly shove what I don't need right now into my locker and close it up. "Look, I've got to get to class." I turn to leave, and she grabs my arm. I try not to flinch but no such luck.

"Hey, Brady, it's me. Are you freaked out that I asked you to the dance?" She lets go of my arm.

"Yeah, kinda sorta. I mean, why would you do that?" I begin walking to class and she walks with me.

"I don't know. I guess I thought since we're best friends it was no big deal. If it freaks you out too much, then just forget it."

I want to take her up on it, but when I glance over at her, she looks like someone who lost their dog. "No. I said yes, so I will go with you."

"Good, because I've never been to a dance before. Oh, and I'm trying out for cheer, too."

"Who are you and what did you do with Danni?" I ask, earning me a laugh.

"I want to try all the girly stuff. You know . . . get it out of the way. I know that you always think of me as one of the guys but I'm here to tell you—there is more to me than that. I've got to get to class. I'll see you after practice later." She races off before I can protest. I take a deep breath and head into class, anticipating the worst. Most people are too busy with their own shit to be focused on mine. Only my teacher, Mr. Foley, gives me a look of pity. That's the look that I dread the most. I use the *I'm going to ignore you* approach and take my seat, making sure to keep myself busy with the stuff in my backpack until class starts. Now I just have to pray I can make it through the rest of my day without any trouble.

Dane

I was able to block out two hours before lunch to meet with Josh. His office being in the next town brought some relief; I knew I wouldn't run into Julie. I pulled up and sat in my car for at least fifteen minutes, staring at a building that looked like it was one step away from being condemned. I don't know what I was expecting, but it wasn't that. My palms were so sweaty from the tight grip I had on the steering wheel. The thought—*I need to trust someone*— was on loop in my head. Finally, after realizing it was now or never, I got out of my car and made my way inside, not sure what awaited me.

The office did not upstage the outside of the building

in appearance. The only receptionist was on the phone, so I waited nervously, bouncing from foot to foot, taking note of my surroundings. *When did I become this person?* I didn't realize I was lost in my own thoughts until the receptionist tried to get my attention.

"*I'm sorry, I was lost in my thoughts.*"

"*You wouldn't be the first one. How may I help you?*" Her smile was comforting.

"*I'm Dane Johnson. I have an appointment with Josh.*" Just as I finished, she got up and instructed me to follow her into an adjoining office that looked like a bomb blew up inside. There was a young guy on the phone behind his desk. He held up a hand, signaling me to wait. I turned to thank the lady just as she was leaving. Josh hung up, came around the desk, and quickly shook my hand. He was young, tall, and very thin—nothing like I had expected.

"*Hey, sorry about that. Abby said you needed my help. She shared a little bit of what she knows of your situation. Have a seat and tell me everything; leave nothing out. No matter how insignificant you think it is, or how embarrassed you are. Everything means something.*"

I had a seat and took a few calming breaths, while he grabbed a pad and took a seat across from me. "*I'm not sure where to start.*"

"*The beginning is always a good place.*" He chuckled and for some reason, I found it calming, not annoying.

"*I guess it would be from when we got together in high school.*" I rehashed everything up to the drunk episode at school the day before. I thought I would have a hard time sharing my story, but I didn't hold back even though he was a stranger.

"Has she hit Brady or sexually abused him?"

The knot in my stomach came back with a vengeance. *"I know she has hit him. I don't think she has sexually abused him but, again, I can't say for sure. I've tried to always be home when they are. Hearing myself say that makes it sound so lame, and makes me feel like such a failure as a parent . . . as a man. I can't seem to find a safe way out of this for him . . . for us."*

"First, you are not a failure. There aren't as many options for men when it comes to domestic violence. Second, my job is to legally find a safe way out for you and Brady. I will, at some point, need to sit down with him. Do you think that will be a problem?"

"I don't know. It's one thing for me to go public with this, but he's a teenager. The teenage years suck to begin with never mind adding this to it. It's got to be his decision." He's tapping his pen on the pad and, for some strange reason, as annoying as it is, I can't seem to pull my eyes away.

"To talk to me, yes, it's his decision, but to get the hell out of the situation—no. You need to remember that you are the adult in the room. I don't say that to be mean; I think you've been abused physically, mentally and, at this point, you're gun shy. Believe it or not; everything you are feeling is normal. Do you have any family or any sort of support from friends?"

"No, my mom passed away from cancer years ago. My dad drank himself to death. I'm an only child. I was in the Navy; they became my family."

"Can you turn to any of your friends from the Navy for help?"

I stared into space, trying to formulate the words, but my embarrassment took over. I had to look away as my face turned red. How could I tell the few friends I've maintained over the years that my wife beats me, and I let her? I'd be labeled a pussy.

"Dane, don't sweat it. We can come back to that later. For now, let's look at your options so we can formulate a plan. The first thing I need to do is meet with Brady. When can we make that happen?"

"I will look at his schedule and let you know. What's next?" Feeling antsy, I just wanted to be done with all of this.

"I will need to file an order of protection for Brady. I'm also going to file a restraining order against Julie, which is why I need to speak to him. At the same time Julie is served with both of them, I'm also going to serve her with divorce papers. While this is happening, you and Brady will be in a safe house. If she flips out, which I suspect she will, you and Brady will be safely tucked away."

I tried to absorb all of this, but I kept seeing Julie flip out. "Is all of this really necessary?"

He put his pen down and with his elbows on his knees, he leaned forward. His jaw seemed tight. "Let me tell you a story that might put this into better perspective for you. There was a man who was in a similar situation as you with one exception: he had two young children under the age of ten. The man was constantly abused, both physically and emotionally. His wife was jealous of anyone he came into contact with. He was a public figure and even though he went to work with scratches all over him—nothing was done. One day the wife snapped and shot the husband in the head before turning the gun on herself. The children, ages six and nine, were in the house at the time. The man was Phil Hartman, the actor. Do you understand what I'm trying to tell you? Every threat, no matter how small, must be taken seriously. You can't think it won't happen to you or Brady. I'm sure Hartman didn't think his wife would go to that extreme, but she did. You hear these things on the news, and you think it could never happen to you. Stuff like that only happens to other people. Trust me, it can happen to anyone."

"Okay, I will talk to Brady today. When all of this is over, will we have to leave town permanently?"

"I'm not sure. But from what you're telling me, when she becomes drunk, she becomes volatile. She can buy liquor and drink whenever she wants, so the odds are not in your favor. My job, Dane, is to prepare you for the worst-case scenario and work off of that. Your job is to be a hundred percent honest with me, no matter how small the detail.

"Okay, let's meet back here in two days. My assistant, Janice, has put together a package for you, detailing everything I will need from you. Do not let Julie see it. You and Brady need to start therapy. I had Janice set up an appointment for tomorrow afternoon for both of you. I know it's hard to get an appointment with any specialist, but she is someone I can send people to in an emergency, and I think this qualifies as one." He got up and lead me out of the office to Janice, waiting with a folder.

"Thank you." I took the folder and made my way outside, my head spinning from information overload. I sat in the car with the A/C blowing and a tight grip on the folder. How the hell did my life spin so far out of control?

CHAPTER FIVE

Brady
One week earlier . . .

ODAY I KEPT MY HEAD DOWN AND TRIED TO stay under the radar. That is, until practice. Coach decided it was time to be all warm and fuzzy. He pulled me aside and decided I needed to know all the perils of getting into a car with a drunk driver. It doesn't matter that the driver was my mother. No one seems to get it, not even my dad. This is my mom—good, bad, or otherwise. How am I supposed to handle her when she's drunk? Yeah, I know don't get into a car when someone is drunk, but that's easier said than done. When she's drunk, she goes off—bad. Dad tries to always be there but that's not always the case. Plus, I have to go to school and try to carry on like nothing is happening. On top of all of the crap I have going on in my life, Danni has turned our friendship upside down. Why the hell did she have to ask me to the dance? Who even goes to these things? This is my life and, right now, it sucks.

She was supposed to meet me after practice but she's late. I'm about to go look for her when I hear my mom yelling out my name, then see her coming toward me. *Ugh.* No time like the present to face the wrath that I'm sure she will throw at me.

"*Hey, Mom.*"

"Don't hey, Mom me. You need to come home now."

I take a few steps closer toward her, trying to figure out if she's drunk. Sometimes it's hard to tell. I don't smell anything, but her eyes are bloodshot. "Mom, I had practice today, remember? Besides, I'm waiting for Danni." Out of the corner of my eye, I see Danni heading towards us.

"I don't really care. We are going home—now. After what happened yesterday, you're grounded indefinitely."

"Okay, just give me a minute to let her know—please. I'll meet you back at the car." I don't wait for an answer. I catch up to Danni before she reaches us. The last thing I need is my mom saying stupid shit to her.

"Hey, my mom is here. I need to go home. She's saying I'm grounded but I'm not sure for how long or even why. I'll call you later." I'm about to leave when she grabs my arm.

"Is she drunk?"

"I don't think so. Look, don't worry; I'll be okay." I pull out of her grasp and hightail it out of there before anything more can happen. I head toward the car. Thankfully, everyone is already gone. The last thing I want is to draw any more attention toward myself. What I really want is for this day to just end already.

Dane

After sitting in my office, trying to let everything Josh said sink in, I decided to get started on the paperwork he gave me only to realize that a lot of what he needed Julie keeps in a firebox in the closet. Passports, Brady's birth certificate, and our marriage certificate. All the stuff that needs to be originals. This meant I had to get all of it out when she wasn't there and hope she didn't have to go into the box for anything. I checked the time; Brady was still at baseball practice. There was an activities bus that he usually took home but if I left at that moment, I was sure I'd get to the school just as practice ended. I needed to talk to him about seeing Josh and figure out what excuse to give Julie. The sooner this is all over, the better.

When I got to the school, I saw Julie's car pulling out of the parking lot with Brady in the back seat. I didn't want him in the car with her. I followed her home. She seemed to be okay, except for the fact that she was driving very slowly. Either she saw me behind her, or she had a drink. I stopped a block from the house and pulled over. Waiting has never been my strong suit. However, I didn't want to show up right behind her. I didn't want to do anything to set her off. The more I think about it, the more I have to agree with Josh about getting therapy. If nothing else, a therapist can help give us some clarity about our situation. After enough time had passed, I went home. I found Brady in his room, headphones on. I waved but he

31

was engrossed in something on his phone. I looked for Julie and found her in the kitchen cooking. Of course, she had a glass of wine next to her. *Why did I never notice this before?* Her drinking was constant and not just when she was out with friends. "Hey, what's for dinner?"

"Why were you following me? Do you think I'm an idiot? Where did you go after I got home?"

Her peppering me with questions kind of threw me off guard. "I went to pick up Brady, but you beat me to it. No big deal. I pulled over because a client called me, needing some information."

She rolled her eyes and went back to chopping peppers. "I'm making stir fry. I got a call from CPS today. That bitch from the school reported me to them. She told them I was drunk and was trying to drive my son home. What business is it of hers anyway? They are coming out here tomorrow at one to talk to me. They said they will be doing a home check at that time."

"When I went to pick up Brady, I tried to talk her out of reporting it, but she said she was obligated to. Besides, there were other witnesses that would have reported it. Why the hell would you drive when you've been drinking? My dad was an alcoholic, so you know the way I feel about it, Julie. Please make me understand why you think it's okay to drive drunk?"

"Oh, for Pete's sake, I had one glass of wine and everyone is making a federal case out of it. I don't give a shit; let them look around all they want. They won't find anything wrong. Dinner will be ready in an hour, and you need to stop being such a stuffed shirt." She continued on with her prep work.

I know when I'm beating a dead horse, and this was one of those times. Instead, I thought while she's busy cooking, it would be a good time to get the documents I needed from the fire box. *"I'm going to jump in the shower before dinner,"* I called out as I headed down the hallway. I suck at lying or even embellishing the truth, so it was best she didn't see my face when I said that. I began sneaking around my closet as if everyone were watching me, when in reality, who really gives a shit that I need my son's birth certificate? I found it and quickly put it in my suitcase before heading into the shower.

It had been a long, mentally taxing day and sometimes those are worse than the physically taxing days. I closed my eyes and let the hot water run down my back. I replayed everything Josh said. *Could Julie be capable of sexually abusing Brady? Could I be that blind?* I felt the bile rise in my throat. I wanted to be wrong about this. I turned the water to ice cold to shock my system before stepping out. When I got out of the bathroom, Julie was standing there. Her eyes traveled up and down my body before she stopped and looked me in the eye.

"This whole mess isn't only my fault, Dane, it's yours too." She placed one hand on her hip and took a step forward.

"My fault?! I'm not the one who is drinking and driving. I've warned you about that numerous times and this time you wanted to put my son in the car with you! You're lucky you're not in jail!"

"Well, if you were a better husband maybe I wouldn't have to have an occasional drink. Hell, I can't even remember the last time we had sex."

"A better husband? I've given you everything, Julie.

A nice house, a great son, I even offered to pay for your schooling—everything. I don't ask you for much; take care of Brady, and the house. That's it. As far as sex is concerned, well dear, that road goes both ways. It's kind of hard to have any physical relationship with someone who is usually passed out. Hell, you don't even take any pride in your appearance anymore. Excuse me if yoga pants and a ripped-up t-shirt don't do it for me." Before I could say anything more, her fist came around toward my face. I reacted quickly and grabbed her wrist but not before her foot came up, hitting me square in my nuts. I dropped to my knees, letting go of her wrist so I could cup my balls to make sure they were still there. *"Bitch."*

She turned and left the room, slamming the door behind her.

Brady

Noise canceling headphones are a wonderful thing. They can drown out the constant fighting that seems to be the norm between my parents. Growing up I used to think there was a monster under my bed. As I got older, I realized the real monster is my mom, and she's right in the next room. I love my parents, but as time goes on, I pity my father and fear my mother. I'd run away if I had someplace to go but, then again, I shouldn't be the one to go. I ask myself every day why my dad takes it. Does he stay because of me? How is any of this helping me? How does it help any of us? My phone suddenly lights up with a text from Danni. *Her timing is always perfect.*

Danni: Making sure you got home okay.

Me: Yeah, but they are at it again.

Danni: I wish you would let me tell my mom what's going on; she would know what to do.

Me: You promised me you wouldn't do that.

Danni: I promised you I would give you time, but it doesn't look like things are getting any better. If anything, they are getting worse. Why won't you let me help?

Me: when are the tryouts for cheer?

Danni: Don't try to change the subject.

Me: I'm tired of talking about it. Now when are the try outs?

Danni: Tomorrow after class. Are you going to be there?

Me: I want to but I'm not sure since I'm grounded. Gotta run. Dinner. TTYL.

Why the heck is she getting all girly? Things were great the way they were. Maybe Dad can help me figure this out. I head into the kitchen and Mom is banging everything she touches. Dad is sitting at the table and looks up from his newspaper. He has a strange look on his face, one I've never noticed before. I'm about to question him when he gives his head a little "no" shake and goes back to his paper. I swear; it's like constant eggshells around here.

"Are you just going to stand there? Grab a plate and get started. I spent enough time out of my day cooking this for you, the least you can do is eat it before it gets cold." My mom's voice snaps me into reality. If I don't grab my food now, she'll throw it away.

"Sorry, thanks for cooking, Mom." Maybe I can kill her with kindness. I quickly fill my plate and have a seat. "Danni has cheer tryouts tomorrow after school. Can I go?" I ask.

She slams her fork down so hard, everything on the table rattles. "What part of you're grounded don't you get?"

"I didn't do anything. So exactly why am I being grounded!?" When she gets angry her right cheek turns bright red. It's when I know to run. Tonight, however, I'm not running. I need to be there for Danni even if I don't understand what's going on with her.

"You didn't get in the car right away. Because of you, CPS is coming here tomorrow. So, you can't go to school; you have to be here when they come."

"What do they want from me?"

"They didn't say you need to be here; I'm telling you I want you here."

"Dad, will you be here?" I turn to him.

She doesn't give him a chance to answer. She starts banging her fists on the table. "There is no reason for him to be here. It's you, Brady, all you. It's always about you."

Before I could reply, my dad finally snaps out of whatever daydream he's been in and jumps into the argument. "Julie, I have no intention on being here when CPS comes tomorrow, and Brady will be going to school."

His voice is loud and bellowing but he doesn't stand a chance against her. Mom picks up her plate and flings it across the table. My dad quickly ducks out of the way. It narrowly misses him. I've lost whatever appetite I had. I get up and put my dish in the sink, leaving them to deal with tomorrow.

Dane

I had gotten quicker at dodging flying plates and body blows from Julie. Well, except for the blow to my balls that I wasn't expecting. *"Listen up, Julie, if you want CPS to think we are one big happy family then it's best if Brady goes to school. Make it seem like it was just a onetime thing and move on. If you have him here it will make you look guilty, like you are putting on a show for their benefit. Let's face it, they are not idiots and they've been around the block before. Besides, I made an appointment for him with a counselor tomorrow, so I'll be dropping him off at school in the morning and picking him up early."* I could literally see the curtain of rage come down on her face. She gripped the sides of the table as I took in a deep breath, waiting for her to lose it.

"Do you really think counseling is going to help this family?" Her voice was barely above a whisper, not what I was expecting.

"I'm willing to try anything. I've offered you an out. I've suggested family counseling for all of us. Everything I suggest, though, you shoot down. I decided not to wait for you to give the okay. I don't want Brady to grow up thinking this is what a normal relationship is!" I was waving my hands around like a deranged person and raising my voice. None of this was me—none of it.

"You can do whatever you want but just keep in mind that I will never, ever give up my son; I'd sooner kill us first.

As long as I'm alive, I will make it my business to keep you miserable."

Her words sent a chill up my spine. All I could think about was the story Josh told me earlier. "Why!? What did I ever do to you? Why would you do this to your son? He's your only child and you couldn't give two fucks about him!"

"You left me behind, Dane. You went into the Navy and made that your world. When you came home, you were different. I was no longer the center of your universe; it was all about Brady. It's still all about Brady. When I wanted another child, you shut that right down; you went out and got a vasectomy. You didn't even tell me! You have your work and you have Brady. What do I have?" she yelled while banging her fist on the table.

"All of this is because I didn't want another child? If we did have another one, what would your excuse be then? You are looking for anything to blame your behavior on. None of this is my fault. You use Brady as a weapon against me. How do you think that makes him feel?" I could see the veins in her neck straining against her skin. Her eyes glanced towards the bread knife on the table. Before she could move, I swiped it off the table and tossed it on the floor. "Not gonna happen. Not while my son is in the house. You hate me; I get it, but how about stepping up to the plate and being a real mom for a change? Do what's best for Brady—walk away." With that I got up and left the room.

CHAPTER SIX

Brady

I TRY NOT TO LISTEN WHEN THEY ARE FIGHTING. But sometimes I can't help it, so I hide in the shadows and listen. Most times it's just my mom screaming like something out of a horror movie. Last night was different. Last night she said she would kill us. I'm scared. Was she serious? I heard my dad tell her he's taking me to a counselor. That's nice, but he didn't say anything to me about it. Danni keeps telling me to talk to her mom. Why would I drag anyone else into this nightmare? It's embarrassing enough that Danni knows. If I tell her what went on last night, she will lose her shit. I couldn't even talk to Danni's mom, now he expects me to talk to a total stranger?!

I get ready for school, but who knows where I'll end up. Maybe I need to put more thought into running away.

I always thought I was the problem, but after their fight last night, I know it's not just me but Dad, too. If I run away, how can I leave him here with her? What if she really tries to kill him . . . kill us both? Maybe she wasn't serious. Maybe she was trying to scare him. She sure did scare me.

There is a tap on my door before it opens, forcing my stomach into knots. It's Dad, thank God.

"Hey, are you ready?"

"Am I really going for counseling?"

"Grab your backpack; we'll talk about it in the car. Did you eat breakfast?"

"No, not much of an appetite this morning," I admit as he pushes the door open further for me to step through.

"We have time; we can drive through McDonalds for breakfast. Maybe by then you'll have an appetite. Besides, I could always use more coffee."

As we head out, I look around for my mom, but she is nowhere in sight. The ride starts out quiet, but I have to know if she was serious last night. "Dad, I heard everything last night." My words hang in the air like a stink that comes from driving over a skunk.

"Everything?"

"Yeah, everything. Was she serious about killing us?" I can't believe I even have to ask this question.

"Honestly, I don't know. If you would have asked me that six months ago, I would have said no. Unfortunately, a lot has changed since then. I think the counseling will be good for both of us. If nothing else, she will have a better understanding of our situation and give us the best advice on how to move forward."

"What are we supposed to tell her?"

"The truth. Tell her everything you've seen and heard. Tell her how you are feeling. Whatever you do, Brady, don't hold back. That wouldn't help either of us."

"So, I'm just supposed to tell this person that I never met before that my mother is a drunk, beats us whenever she wants, and has now threatened to kill us. How is that going to help us?" I ask just as he pulls through the drive thru. He orders and after getting our food, parks the car. He turns toward me, and for the first time, I see that my dad looks like a beaten man. Not physically, because those bruises are always out of sight, but in every other way that counts.

"Brady, I don't know how or if this is going to help us, but I'm willing to try anything to get us out of this situation. I've also met with an attorney who specializes in these types of situations. He would like to meet with you tomorrow. I need you to keep all of this to yourself. The less your mom knows, the better."

"Wow, you've always told me to be honest. Now you're asking me to hide stuff from Mom. What's going to happen if she finds out?"

"I venture to say that she will take it out on me like she always does. However, I can't guarantee that she won't take it out on you too. I need you safe. So please, for both our safety, please keep everything to yourself. Don't even tell Danni."

Crap, now I have to keep this from my best friend? I just lost my desire to finish my breakfast. I put it all back in the bag and pass it to him. "I need to get to school." He takes the bag. The rest of the ride is in silence.

When I get to school, Danni is waiting for me at my locker. I drop my backpack and work on my lock. I glance over to her and she's glaring at me, like she's waiting for me to spill whatever I'm hiding. I can't hide anything from her. Besides, I know this is too huge to even try. "My dad is picking me up at lunch for a doctor's appointment." I hold my hand up, stopping her before she can start the usual Danni inquisition. "It's just a physical that I need for the team." Sadly, the lies are becoming easier.

"You didn't say anything before about it?"

"My mom made the appointment and forgot about it, of course. That's why my dad is taking me." She says nothing, just staring at me. God, I hope she believes me.

"Okay, I'll let you know what happens with the tryouts."

"I'm sorry. I really wanted to be there for you. I have to get this done, though. I'll call you tonight." I grab my backpack and quickly head to class before she can ask me anything more.

Right before lunch I'm called to the front office. I figured it's my dad picking me up but instead I see my mom standing by the desk in the office. Luckily, her back is to the door, so she doesn't see me. I turn to take off and almost crash right into Ms. Scott who is behind me.

"Brady, is everything okay?"

Crap, what do I tell her? "Ms. Scott, please hide me, now!" I beg. She takes my arm and we take off at a quick pace down the hall. We duck into the stairwell.

"Brady, now why don't you tell me what's going on?"

My mom saying, she would kill us keeps replaying in my head. I know it's now or never and I have to trust someone. I just don't know what to do.

"Brady, I promise you; you can trust me."

"You say that but if you didn't report her to CPS, this would not be happening, so how can I trust you? How can I trust anyone?"

"I had no choice, Brady. I have to do what is best for you. Please tell me why you need to be hidden from your mother?"

I take a deep breath and blurt out everything from the counselor to my mom saying she would kill us. Ms. Scott never even blinks. "I know I shouldn't go with her. I know my dad has an appointment for me and he is supposed to be the one to pick me up. He doesn't want me in the car with her. I don't know what to do."

"Follow me, Brady, and be quiet." We race down the steps, ending up in the basement, which I didn't even know existed.

"It's creepy down here; are you sure you know where you're going?"

"Yes. There are steps just past the boiler room that lead out to the back of the building. It's where the maintenance stores all of their equipment. When we get there, you stay inside and call your dad. Tell him to meet us at Josh's office. He will know where that is. I'll get my car and come around back to pick you up."

"Okay." We reach the door and she guides me behind the stairwell before she races outside. I feel like I'm missing something. Normally, I wouldn't think that. I usually ignore all the drama at home, but after that argument last night and my dad hiding shit from me, who the hell knows? I shouldn't have to be thinking about this shit. I should be worrying about practice and why my best friend is getting all girly on me. I pull out my phone and start texting my dad.

Me: Mom tried to pick me up at school. She didn't see me. I ran into Ms. Scott. She had me go with her. She said for you to pick me up at Josh's office. She said you would know where that is. Dad, who's Josh and what is going on?

Dane: Stay with Ms. Scott. Brady, you can trust her. She will keep you safe. I'm on my way and I'll explain everything when I get there.

The door swings open and Ms. Scott rushes in. I don't have time to think. She leads me out the door and into her running car. She makes me duck my head down so no one can see me. I count the speed bumps; I know when I get to five, I'm out of the parking lot. "Can I come up now?"

"Yeah, sorry about that. It's lunch time and there are a lot of people mulling about."

I lift my head up and we are on some back roads I've never heard of. "Do you do this a lot?"

"By this, do you mean saving you from getting hurt or possibly killed?" she asks. I just stare at her. "I've helped some people, and some people have helped me. After what you told me about your mom threatening to kill everyone, I couldn't take the chance of a confrontation. Hell, I don't even know if she was sober. I was not about to let you walk into that situation."

"Who is Josh?" She smiles at this question and it kind of makes me relax a little.

"Josh is my big brother. He's an attorney. He practices family law and helps people that need it. He helped me when I was in a similar situation. Brady, you can trust him."

"What do you mean you were in a similar situation?"

"I was married, and my husband abused me. He would hit me in places that no one would see. I thought there was no way out. I really thought no one would believe me. He made me feel like I deserved it. I felt like I couldn't do anything right. He beat me so bad that I lost my eye. My brother got me out of the situation, and I moved here. I trusted him with my life, Brady, and you can too."

"Wait, you lost your eye?"

"Of course, all of that and you want to know about my eye. Yes, I have a glass eye."

"Wow, you can't even tell. What happened to your husband?"

"He went to jail. We are here."

That's it—conversation over. My dad pulls up as we get out of the car. "Thank you, Ms. Scott." I climb into his car, but he gets out to talk to Ms. Scott. They don't talk long before he's back in the car. "Okay, Dad, now what is going on?"

"Your, mom doesn't want us to go to counseling. She was determined for you to be home today when CPS comes. I told her I already picked you up. That's all I told her. Now, we are going to the counselor and after that, we are going to see Josh. He's our attorney. We were supposed to see him tomorrow but things with your mom seem to be escalating."

"Are we going to have to move away? Ms. Scott said she had to."

"What else did she tell you?"

"Just that her brother helped her, and he can be trusted."

"Oh, okay. I don't know if we will have to move away. But understand this, Brady, if it means you will be safe, then we move. Your mom never talked about killing us before. That was a game changer. No matter what, whatever it takes, we are a team for life."

Something tells me my life will never be the same again.

CHAPTER SEVEN

COUNSELING IS VERY INTERESTING. IT'S nothing like you see on TV. This lady, Miss Thomas, hardly talks; I'm expected to do the talking. My dad and I went in together. That was okay because he did most of the talking, but then she wanted to talk to me alone. I don't know what she thinks I have to add to this mess. Hell, when I'm not getting beat up, I'm usually hiding in my room.

"Brady, does your mother hit you?"

"Isn't that why we are here? Yes, she hits me when my dad is not around. She hits me in places no one would think to look."

"Has she ever touched you in a way that made you uncomfortable?"

"No! Never." What the Hell? I just want out of here.

"Brady, if she did, it's not your fault. None of this is

your fault. Is there anything you want to share with me today?"

"I don't want to move. I have my friends here and I finally made the team."

"What sport do you play?"

"Baseball. It took me two tries to make the team. The first time, coach kept me in the secondary. But I practiced all summer and this year I made it. I play shortstop and I've got a good batting average." She's writing on her pad and then puts everything down on the table next to her. I really want to see what she wrote but I don't think that will happen.

"Are you only worried about moving away?"

"Well hell, when you put it that way, I sound like a spoiled brat. I'm worried about my dad, too. I just want a normal life. Is that so much to ask?"

"No, it's not, but since the situation has escalated, things might change very quickly. I need you to be prepared for that. You will be meeting with Josh later, and he will put together a plan. Tell him your fears and let him figure out a plan that will work for you and your dad. Your current situation is not safe, Brady. You and your dad need to be safe. Everything else that follows after that, I'll help you deal with."

Miss Thomas had me put her phone number in my phone. She said I could call her anytime and if she wasn't there, hang up and call 911. All of this is very easy to say, but when you're living in this hell, it's very hard to do. As quick as this started is as quick as it ended. Now, we are on our way to meet with Josh.

"Dad, what are we going to tell mom when we get home?"

"She knew I was picking you up today. She really can't say anything. There is nothing wrong with going for counseling. Besides, she had CPS to deal with today."

"Can they take me out of the house?"

"No, I don't think so, but that's a good question for Josh. Is that what you're worried about?"

I'm trying not to look at him. I don't want him to see how worried I actually am. "I don't want to move away, Dad. I just want the beatings to stop for both of us. Maybe mom should be the one to get some help."

"She has to want to get help. We can't force her into it. I know, I've tried. Come on, we are here." We park the car and head into a building that looks abandoned.

A very tall man steps into the room and introduces himself as Josh. He looks like Ms. Scott, only taller. Her words keep playing in my head: *Brady, you can trust him.* Dad tells him everything that went down last night, including her threatening to kill us as well as her showing up at school today when she wasn't supposed to.

"Wow, it sounds like things are escalating. We need to get a handle on this now. Brady, did you get a close look at your mom at school today? Do you think she was drinking?"

"No, her back was toward the door. I don't know if she was drinking or not. I saw her and started to back away. I ran into your sister, Ms. Scott. She got me safely out of the school. My mom was not supposed to pick me up, my dad was. I was surprised to find her there. Look, I don't want to move away. I shouldn't have to." I blurt it out, so everyone knows I'm not leaving.

"Brady, you might have to move for a little bit, just until we get the situation under control. Remember, nothing is forever. Dane, I'd like to talk to Brady for a few minutes. There is fresh coffee in the waiting room." Dad doesn't question him; he just ups and leaves. Why is it everyone wants to talk to me alone?

"Brady, I get why you don't want to leave. You've got some good friends, baseball, and, besides that, this is the only place you've ever known. I will do my best for you, I promise. Has your mom ever mentioned killing either of you before last night?"

"No. Last night was the first time, but I don't always listen when they are fighting. Most times, I put on my headset and play my video games. They are a lot better than real life."

"I love video games; they help me forget about the world. Which ones do you like?"

"Fortnite is my favorite. I also like Call of Duty and Madden NFL. What about you?"

"Fortnite; I'm so addicted. You know, whether you think your mom was serious or not, I still have to treat it like she is. I know this is a difficult question, but I have to ask it. Just know nothing leaves this room. Has she ever touched you in a way that a mother shouldn't, a way that made you uncomfortable?"

"This is the second time today I've been asked this question. The answer is the same: no. She has punched me in my back and my stomach, but she's never done anything else." Maybe there are monsters out there that are worse than her.

"Okay, we will leave it at that. Now, I need to

formulate a plan. Let's get your dad in here and get started."

This gave me a weird feeling, like my life was about to be changed forever and I'm just along for the ride.

CHAPTER EIGHT

W E HEAD TOWARD HOME WITH A PLAN. I'M not sure about it, but Dad thinks it will work out. "Dad, are you sure this is a good plan?"

"I don't think your mother meant what she said. I think it was said out of frustration. I think Josh getting the restraining order and filing for emergency custody is a good thing. From there, we can try to come to an agreement. I know Josh wanted us in a safe house tonight, but I think it will just escalate the situation. I just want us safe. I want to live a normal life. One that we could both be proud of. Maybe we can end this civilly and we won't have to move."

"Dad, Josh said we should be prepared for the worst, but it doesn't sound like you think the worst is going to happen."

"I just don't think she would do anything like that. I think she needs help and that's what I want to try and do, get her the help she needs."

"Why wouldn't Josh try to get her some help?"

"He wants to, but he wants us out of the house first. I think if we did that, it would make matters worse."

I don't say anything. I mean, he's my father, so I guess I should believe him. After all, he would know her the best. "Oh, Dad, did you know that Ms. Scott has a glass eye?" His eyes grow wide. I guess that means no.

"Well, that was out of left field. No, son. That's pretty personal information. Did she share that with you, or is it part of the typical junior high rumor mill?"

"Yeah, she shared it with me. I'm thinking I should keep it to myself, though."

"I suggest you do. I'm sure it's not something she wants broadcasted all around the school, the same way you don't want what we're going through all around the school."

"Good point. I missed practice today. I'm going to need a note for the coach. I'll have to stay late and make up the time I lost."

"I'll take care of it when we get home. Were you comfortable with Miss Thomas? Do you think you want to keep seeing her?"

"Maybe. I'll let you know." I probably should have asked her about Danni and why she's getting all girly on me. If I have to see her, I might as well get something out of it.

When we pull up to the house, every light is on. Every day it's a struggle figuring out which mother will be home. When we get inside, music is going, and Mom is in the kitchen cooking. Maybe things will be okay. I mean, there's always hope—right? "Hi, Mom," I greet her. Dad walks in behind me and puts a hand on my shoulder. Maybe he's also wondering which mom will show up.

"Brady, I went to school to pick you up today, but you were already gone."

Before I can answer dad squeezes my shoulder and pulls me back a little.

"Julie, I told you we were going to counseling today."

"I know that. I just thought it was after school. I wanted him here when CPS came."

Even I remember Dad telling her we wouldn't be here, and I wasn't paying that close attention to them fighting.

"How did it go?" Dad asks.

I take a step around Dad and head to the fridge for a drink. I don't want either of them to think I care one way or the other. Besides, Dad already knows how I feel. I just want to make sure I can stay here.

"I assured them I was fine, that it was a reaction from some cold medication. They looked around and they must have liked what they saw. They said they will come back tomorrow to talk to Brady. If that goes okay, then they will do a recheck in six months. If there are no other incidents after that, they will close the case. I'm sure they have better things to do with their time. I guess you should have let him be here since they wanted to talk to him. Once again, Dane, you made a big mess for me to clean up."

"Did they leave their contact information?"

"Of course, they did. I knew you would be all over it, so I left it on your desk. Now, can we put an end to all of this?"

I nearly choke on my Gatorade. This whole mess was her doing. "I've got homework to do. I'll be in my room." I quickly make my exit before Dad blows up. I don't want to be a part of any of this. My room is my sanctuary. It's the only place I don't feel like I'm walking on eggshells. When I'm safely inside, I notice all of my stuff has been moved around. No doubt she wanted it clean for the show she had to put on. I'm not in here five minutes and I can already hear the yelling. I'm hunting around for my headphones. Where the hell could she have put them? The yelling is getting louder. I do the only thing I can right now to get away from the noise, I go into my closet, close the door, and turn up the music on my phone. These are the times I really need my best friend. I want to call her, but I know she will want me to tell her mom everything. I'm not ready for that. I wish I could be anywhere but here.

Dane

"Julie, Brady did very well with the counseling today, we both did. I think we could all benefit from it. We could get this family back on track. I'm willing to do whatever it takes. Won't you just try one session—please? If you hate it after that, then you don't have to go back." I wasn't opposed to begging if it would've turned her around.

"You're making some really big assumptions here, Dane. You think I want a life with you. Haven't you figured it out,

yet? I hate you! Why would I ever want to spend the rest of my life in this self-imposed hell that I've found myself in?!"

She stormed out of the kitchen and into the family room. I followed close behind her. I clenched my hands while I felt the adrenaline rushing through every inch of my body. My throat went dry and I wanted to scream. *"Then, why are you here? Answer me, Julie! Why the fuck don't you just leave? I've offered you everything, but you just. Won't. Go!"*

"If I leave, then you get Brady. Let's face it; that's all you really want, all you ever wanted from me—a son. You could not give two shits about me. You built your life around Brady and just tossed me aside. I'll never let you have him, ever!"

"How could you say that? I gave up everything for you!"

"You gave up everything for me? For me, Dane?! What fucking planet are you on? I gave up going away to college. I stayed home and took care of Brady while you were out playing sailor; you couldn't even get that right. You're pathetic, Dane, a pathetic excuse for a man. There is no way in hell I'll ever let you have Brady. I'd kill him first . . . right in front of you to boot. So, think about that one." She paced around the kitchen like a caged animal, screaming so loudly that the veins in her neck were bulging.

"You're a vindictive little bitch. I'm taking Brady out of here tonight and don't you dare try to stop me." I realized then that I was gravely mistaken when I thought we could somehow end this civilly. That she didn't mean what she had said. I turned to leave and made it into the kitchen. That's when I heard it, the swoosh of a baseball bat. I tried to lean out of the way, but it still connected with the side of my head. I could feel something wet trickling down the

side of my face. It only took a minute for me to realize it was blood. She pulled the bat back again to take another swing. I tried to block the blows while trying to grab her hands, but I couldn't. My vision was starting to blur. I fell backwards, hard. *"Julie, please stop, please!"* I begged. That's when I saw Brady out of the corner of my eye. "Brady, stay away!" I yelled.

He started screaming at Julie. "Mom, put my bat down! Leave him alone!"

"Mind your damn business, Brady. Your father deserves what he gets."

She pulled the bat back to swing again. I scrambled to my feet and stepped in front of her. I was very dizzy and grabbed the counter to steady myself. I guess Brady saw the bat coming towards me. He grabbed a knife off the counter, stepped in front of me and then took a step toward Julie. He plunged the knife into her side. She still got off her swing and hit Brady in the head. They both collapsed, Julie landing on top of him. The knife still stuck in her side. I crawled over to them and pushed Julie off of Brady. My hands were shaking so bad; I couldn't find a pulse. *"Come on, Brady, come on. You need to hang on."* I grabbed my phone.

"911, what's your emergency?"

"My wife just beat my son with a baseball bat. She hit him in the head. He's bleeding and I'm not sure if he's breathing. My hands are shaking so bad I can't find a pulse. Help him, please!" I pleaded with the operator. She began giving me instructions, but I couldn't focus on them. Instead, I scooped him up and ran to the car. I told the operator what hospital I was going to and for her to send an

ambulance for Julie. I raced through the streets. Brady
started to moan. *"That's good, Brady. Hang on; we're almost
to the hospital."* I pulled up to emergency, almost driving
right through the glass doors. Two nurses were waiting
with a gurney. They whisked Brady away, but another
nurse held me back.

*"Let the doctors work on him while you tell me what
happened."*

"I want to be with my son."

*"You will be but right now, I need as much information
from you as possible. It could be what helps save him. I need
his medical information."* Her voice was raised enough that
I stopped, realizing she was trying to help us. She began
asking me questions. Everything was like a blur, though.
I told her what I knew. She touched the side of my head
with some gauze, causing me to flinch. Not from the pain
but from the touch. It was an instant reminder of what
went down.

"Press this to your head." She leaned in, her tone soft.
Somehow, I felt she understood it wasn't her touch.

"When can I see my son?"

*"Soon. Now, why don't you tell me what happened
tonight?"*

This is when it hit me that Brady could be in a world
of trouble. It didn't matter that it was self-defense. I don't
trust the system. I don't trust anyone. *"I came home from
work to find her beating Brady. I grabbed the first thing I
could, which was a knife, and stopped her. I called 911, but
they were taking too long. I put Brady in my car and raced
here. He's an innocent boy, caught in the middle of my nightmare."* I'm not a good liar—never was—but I would sell

my soul to the devil himself if it meant my son was kept out of this.

"Has your wife done this before?"

"You mean try to kill my son? No, but she has beaten us with her fist." I hear myself utter the words out loud and they seem fake.

"Why did you stay?"

I stared into space, asking myself that same question. I know the answer but trying to put it into words so that someone else might understand it is very difficult. "Ma'am, it's very easy to assume anyone male or female in this situation could just leave. Unfortunately, it's not that easy. Fear plays a big part in it. Who would believe a big guy like me can't stop a small woman like Julie? I was taught to never raise my hands to a woman, so I tried other things. I even went so far as to offer her everything she could ever want if she would just leave. She refused. She threatened to tell the authorities that I beat her, not the other way around. Who do you think the cops would believe? She threatened to take my son away. I was working with an attorney to find a safe way out of this nightmare, when all of this happened. So, to answer your question, who would believe me and how could I leave and still keep my son safe?"

"I'm sorry you've had to go through this and that you thought you were alone throughout it all. There are agencies that can help. They would believe you. However, you need to take the first step, no matter how scared you are." She opened her desk drawer, pulled out a pamphlet and passed it to me.

"What's this for?"

"I know at times you might think you have no way out, that you are alone in this, but you are not. There are agencies *that can help you and that's one of them. They have programs for male victims and same-sex partner victims. Reach out to them."*

The door to the emergency room opened and a nurse came out. *"Mr. Johnson, the doctor needs to talk to you. Please follow me."* I thanked the nurse and shoved the pamphlet into my pocket as I followed her to my son. When we got to his bed, I had to grab the side rail to steady myself. He was so pale and his little body almost lifeless. I know he thinks he's all grown up; thirteen going on thirty. At that age, I thought the same thing. However, he's not all grown up, he's still my little boy and he always will be.

"Hi, Mr. Johnson, I'm Doctor Cantwell. I'm taking care of your son."

"How is he?"

"He has a skull fracture. When his skull fractured, a sharp fragment of bone cut through one of the blood vessels. The blood collected and caused an epidural hematoma. It looks like the blow was to his temple, which is common in sports-related injuries. I need to surgically remove the epidural hematoma and drain any blood. We need you to sign some papers first." He rattled through all the worst-case scenarios but all I could focus on was my son needed this to survive. With a trembling hand, I quickly sign everything.

I leaned in and whispered in his ear. *"I don't know if you can hear me, but fight like hell, Brady. I love you."* He was then whisked away, instantly leaving me alone and praying for my son's survival. You know it's been said that a watched pot never boils. No truer words were ever spoken. Finally, when I thought I couldn't take it any longer, Dr. Cantwell came into the waiting room and took me into a small room.

"Good news, Mr. Johnson, the hit on Brady's head was not direct. I was able to make a small hole and aspirate the hematoma. He will remain heavily sedated until the swelling starts to go down. After that, we will determine if he has sustained any permanent brain damage. If you have no questions right now, the best thing for Brady is rest. As soon as he's in his room, the nurse will come and get you. I'll check back later." He put his hand out to shake mine before he left. Once again, I was alone and waiting.

CHAPTER NINE

Present Day . . .

THE POLICE HAVE COME AND GONE. I TOLD them I wanted my attorney, so that will buy me some time. All I can do is sit by Brady's bed and listen to the continuous beeping. The doctor said everything went well. They have put him on antiseizure medications, but he's not sure how long he will remain on them. He needs rest, so his brain can have time to heal. I asked the nurse about Julie. She said the doctors removed her spleen, and she will be fine. She offered to stay with Brady if I wanted to see my wife. That's the last thing I want to do. I wish she would have died. I hate myself for feeling like that. I thanked her but declined.

"Mr. Johnson, I know you said you didn't want to be interrupted but your attorney is outside and insisting on speaking with you."

"Thank you. Can you stay with Brady for a few minutes?"

"Yes. I have some stuff to do here anyway. I'll come get you if anything changes."

I step outside but leave the door cracked, so I can hear the constant beeping. Josh is pacing and Abby has a blank stare on her face. I remember my conversation with Brady about her eye, and now I wonder if this has brought back all her bad memories. Have I screwed up another person's life, not just Brady's? Josh rushes over as soon as he sees me. "Please tell me you didn't speak to the police."

"I told them I stabbed Julie to stop her from beating Brady. They said the evidence doesn't match the scene. After that, I told them I wanted my lawyer. I also told the intake nurse the same story. I'm sorry I didn't believe you that things could escalate this quickly. I really didn't believe she had it in her to be that evil." I wrap my arms around my stomach, trying to stop the urge to puke. *Why didn't I listen? Why did I think I was right?* I couldn't even find a way out of this mess, yet, I believed she wouldn't take it to the next level. As I'm listening to the beeping, I realize I've lost all respect for myself. I think I will beat myself up over this for the rest of my life.

Abby steps closer to me and, with a trembling hand, squeezes my shoulder.

"Can I sit with Brady while you talk to Josh?"

"Yes, of course," I reply quickly. She heads inside and Josh motions for me to come closer.

"I got a temporary protection order. I need you to tell me step by step what happened. Remember, what you say to me is privileged." His voice is low. I take a deep breath and try to say the words he needs to hear, but I choke on the bile rising in my throat. How do I say my thirteen-year-old boy picked up a knife and plunged it into his mother? I know *circumstances and all*, but still, it's hard to wrap my mind around it. I finally lean into him and whisper "I didn't stab her; Brady did. He was trying to protect me. I don't want any of this to get out. It will ruin his life. He didn't ask for any of this. We chose to bring him into the world. Unfortunately, my world became his nightmare. Now, I need to protect him at all costs."

"You need to stop looking at it as your fault. You are both the victims in this situation. Brady acted in self-defense, Dane. Don't think for a minute that he purposefully stabbed his mother. I knew you were in denial when you left my office this afternoon. That's why I started the paperwork for the order of protection right away. I think even if I had pushed you harder you wouldn't have believed me. I don't blame you. I've been doing this for years. I've seen hundreds of cases. You have only seen one and it's been from the inside, looking out. It's natural to have disbelief. We don't want to think the people we love are capable of such madness but, unfortunately, they are. Now, I checked on Julie before I came here. She is out of surgery and will be fine. She was assigned a public defender and I served him with the order of protection on her behalf. I hired private security for Brady. They will be here shortly."

The mention of security snaps me back to the reality of our situation. "Do you think she would try to see Brady?"

"From now on, please believe everything I tell you. I would not put it past her to try and play the victim card.

Really, that's her only defense. She will say that you beat Brady. She will also say that you stabbed her when she tried to stop you. Until Brady is able to tell what really happened, all we have is two sides to the story, yours and hers. Brady holds the truth card."

"Why do we have to put him through this? Why can't I just say that I stabbed her?"

"Do you want her to get custody of Brady? Think about that one."

The urgency to vomit takes over. I race to the closest trash can but it's only dry heaves. I straighten up and turn to face Josh, who hands me a few tissues to wipe my mouth. I let out a big sigh of disbelief. "Tonight, I finally started to realize how evil she really is and what lengths she will go to when it comes to hurting me. We can't let her get anywhere near Brady, ever!"

"I'm going to do everything I can to prevent that, Dane," he assures me.

We walk back to Brady's room and I notice someone outside his door. When I get closer, he introduces himself as Brady's security. My mind is racing: this guy is a complete stranger; I don't know anything about him! I just take a deep breath and remind myself that Josh has the good sense to check the guy's credentials. "What do we do next?" I ask Josh.

"You do nothing but take care of your son. I will handle whatever else needs to be done. Do not talk to anyone about this. I'll be in touch." I watch him leave and, for the first time, I feel hopeful. When I get back into the room, Abby is still by Brady's bedside. She has her iPad out and she's reading to him.

"Thanks for staying with him while Josh and I got things worked out."

"No worries. Nothing has changed. I was reading him *Harry Potter and The Chamber of Secrets*. He had mentioned to me that it was one of his favorite books."

How did I not know that? Was I so wrapped up in my own life that I didn't even know my son's favorite book?

"Why don't you read to him for a bit." She passes me her iPad, and for the first time, I notice the scars on her wrists. She must notice me looking and quickly pulls at the hem of her sleeves. I remember Brady telling me about her glass eye. What kind of hell she must have been through. This must be triggering stuff for her while she's witnessing ours?

"Abby, I'm sorry if any of this has brought up some bad memories for you."

"Please, Dane, don't worry about me. I'm happy I got you to Josh. I only wish it was sooner. I know he will help you both. I'll always be here for you if you need me—promise."

We both jump at the slight moan that comes from Brady. Abby rushes out to get the nurse while I practically stick my face in his, willing him to open his eyes.

"Mr. Johnson, please step back so I can get a look at him." I realize the nurse is next to me, gently pulling my arm back. I back up as I pray for him to open his eyes.

"Come back to me Brady, please." I barely croak out the words when Brady opens his eyes! He looks around the room and then his eyes flutter and close. "No, no, no, Brady, come back!"

"Mr. Johnson, give him some time. This is a good sign.

He's fighting his way back home to you." While the nurse makes all kinds of notes and checks the many different machines helping my son, Abby and I just stare at him, waiting for something . . . anything. The nurse calling my name snaps me out of my fog. "I'm sorry I spaced out for a moment."

"Mr. Johnson, I said I called the doctor; he will be here shortly."

Not much time passes before Dr. Cantwell comes in and talks to the nurse as he examines Brady.

"Mr. Johnson, everything looks good. I like the way he is progressing. I will decrease the meds that are keeping him sedated and let him slowly come out of it."

"Are you sure that's the right thing to do?"

"Yes, I've been doing this a long time; I know what I'm doing." He gives me an encouraging smile.

"What do I need to do for him?"

"Let him rest and heal. Right now, that's the best medicine. You look like you could use some rest, too. I know you won't leave. There is a reclining chair in the corner, and I'll have some blankets brought in here for you. I'll be here all night, so I'll keep a close eye on him. Your lawyer informed the hospital about the added security. I'll have a chair put outside the door for him, too. Let me know if there is anything else I can do to help." I'm amazed how compassionate and understanding everyone is.

"Dane, do you want me to get you some food or a change of clothes?" I don't know why I'm so amazed that Abby is still here.

"Thank you. I'll be okay. It's getting late; you should get going."

"I'll leave you my iPad. Maybe it's wishful thinking but reading to him seems to have a calming effect. I'll check back in the morning." She squeezes my shoulder before heading out the door. I open up the iPad and begin reading. Hoping somehow Brady can hear me and gets lost in an incredible story.

CHAPTER TEN

Brady

I COULD HEAR MY DAD TALKING. THE MORE HE talked, the more I realized he was reading my favorite Harry Potter book. I try to talk but nothing comes out. I fought hard to open my eyes, and when I did, the light was so bright that I quickly closed them. At least I'm back in my own body now. It was freaky being on the outside looking in. I wish I could ask my dad why. Why did he lie? What made mom snap? Was it because I went to counseling or was it something with CPS? I just wish I knew why she hates us so much, why she hates me. Did I mess up her life so much that this is the only way out for her? I feel like I'm floating in the ocean. Every time I try to reach the top, it's like a weight pulling me under. *Please, Dad, don't give up on me, not yet.*

Dane

Two days have passed, and nothing with Brady has changed. I have not left his side; I never will. Julie, on the other hand, is being discharged today. Even though they already know, I reminded security that Julie is not permitted anywhere near Brady. There is a light tap on the door before it opens and Abby walks in. I'm happy to see her. She has a calming effect on me.

"Hi, Dane, I brought you a change of clothes. I had to guess on the size, but I think I did okay. I also picked up some toiletries for you." She smiles, passing me a large bag.

"Wow, that was so nice of you." I'm taken aback by her kindness. I'm not used to being looked after.

"I can sit with him while you freshen up," she offers. Before I can protest, she takes the iPad and picks up where I left off in the story.

I'm in the bathroom getting cleaned up when I hear a lot of yelling. I run out of the bathroom and find Julie being pushed in a wheelchair by her best friend Janelle. She's trying to get into the room. Janelle stops pushing the chair as the security guard tries to pull both of them back. If I didn't see it for myself, I wouldn't believe it. "Julie, go away. You know you can't be here. Leave right now or I'm calling the police!" Her eyes are running up and down my body and I realize I'm half undressed.

"So, Dane, are you fucking Brady's guidance counselor now? Are you doing it in front of our son?!"

Abby gets up and pulls the curtain around Brady's bed closed. Thankfully, she stays behind the curtain with him. Not that it matters since the entire floor could probably hear her. "I'm not even going to dignify that with an answer. Get out now or I'm calling the police."

"You can't stop me from seeing my son. I will tell them what you did. I will tell everyone, Dane, that you are a wife beater and worse than that—a child abuser. That's right, Dane, I will tell the world what you've done behind closed doors. What you continue to do. Hell, I've already told your work and now I'm off to tell the police. Janelle, get me the hell out of here, now!"

I follow her out of the room into the hallway, which is bustling with hospital staff. I'm shocked but I shouldn't be. A veil of pure evil washes over her face. *I can't believe she got her friend Janelle to dress up as a nurse.* She's still screaming at me, calling me all sorts of names. The worst part is a few of the nurses are staring at me. They can't possibly believe the rantings of a sick woman. I watch Julie head to the elevator. The doors open and as Janelle wheels her in, she turns and gives me the most sinister smile. If I didn't know then, I sure know now; Josh was right. Everything will hinge on what Brady tells the police. While I was outside the room, two nurses slipped in to check on Brady. I step back into the room; their focus is on the beeping machines. They are looking everywhere but at me. "I'm sorry, everyone, that you had to witness that. Please understand she's a liar. Think about this; why would the judge issue an order of protection for my son against his mother?" The only thing I can hear in the room is the constant beeping of the machines monitoring Brady. I head back into the bathroom and quickly finish getting cleaned up. When I step back into the room, the curtain around Brady's bed is open and Josh is here talking to Abby.

"Well you just missed Julie's performance. As you predicted, she's turning all the blame on me. She said she called my work and told them I'm a wife and child abuser. Is there anything you can do to save my job?"

"I already went to human resources and laid everything out for them, showing them the order of protection. They can't fire you without cause. I also informed the superintendent at Brady's school. I've got you covered; you just need to take care of Brady. Has there been any change?"

"He opened his eyes for a few seconds, but that was it. The doctor said he is progressing nicely. Now it's just a waiting game." If Josh is concerned or disappointed, his face gives nothing away.

"If Julie tries anything again, please don't engage her. The more scenes she creates, the worse it is for her. I venture to say her next move is to file charges against you. Don't worry, I'm prepared for it. Stay here and take care of your son. If anything else happens, call me." He gives me a firm handshake.

"Dane, I'm going to walk Josh to the elevator. I'll be right back," Abby says as Josh turns to leave. I give her a nod. They head out, leaving me alone with Brady.

I sit on the edge of his bed and take his hand. "Hey, buddy, I don't know if you can hear what's been going on, but I need you to forget everything and just focus on getting better. I need you to fight hard, Brady. I know you can do that." I keep staring at him, hoping for something—anything—but he remains very still. I'm left waiting.

As I hold on tight to his hand, I close my eyes and say a prayer. I'm not a religious man but right now, I will take help from anywhere I can get it, even from a god I don't know exists. Abby comes back into the room, biting on her lip. She seems different. It makes me wonder what Josh said to her. "Hey, is everything okay?"

"Does it show?" She winces.

"Yeah."

"My brother is worried about me. Nothing for you to worry about."

"But I am worried. I'm worried that I've dragged you into my hell and it's bringing back memories for you," I admit.

She pulls a chair closer to me and sits down. "Dane, my nightmares will never go away. I've gotten them to a point where they don't rule my life anymore. Josh is worried that I might slip backwards. Truth be told, he has every right to worry. But I can't stop living because of fear. If I do that, then I'm not living at all. I like you, Dane, and I've become very fond of Brady. I'm willing to deal with my past when it creeps into my present, if it means I can help you both."

"Abby, I know nothing about you, yet, I feel like I've known you my whole life. How is that even possible?" She smiles and for the first time I notice her eyes are very blue. I think back to my conversation with Brady and now I'm wondering which eye is glass.

"When Brady is better, we can swap life stories, but I can assure you mine is very boring."

Still holding tightly on to Brady's hand, I suddenly feel him squeeze mine. "Abby, get the nurse; he's squeezing my hand!" Abby jumps up right away and runs out to get the nurse. All I can do is watch Brady squeeze my hand. For the first time, I'm feeling hopeful.

"Brady, can you open your eyes?" Nothing . . .

The nurse rushes in with Abby following quickly behind her. "Has he opened his eyes yet or said anything to you?"

"Ma'am, I asked him if he can open his eyes, but nothing happened. He does have a tight grip on my hand." The nurse tries to take his hand from mine but he's not letting go. His grip is so tight that his fingers are turning white!

"Brady, my name is Connie. I'm your nurse. Can you let go of your dad's hand, please?" The three of us are staring at my hand and finally, Brady loosens his grip. It hits me he can hear me. I wonder if he heard his mother earlier. The thought makes my stomach tighten and the bile rises in my throat. "Brady, that's great. Now, can you try to open your eyes?" He slightly opens them but quickly squeezes them shut. *Why won't he keep them open?* "Good job, Brady. Does the light bother you? Squeeze my hand if it does." He squeezes her hand. Nurse Connie quickly dims the lights. "Brady, I know the light is bothering you, but I just need to take a quick look at your eyes with my little flashlight." She pulls a pen-like object off the neckline of her scrub top and turns it on, revealing its true identity. "Okay, bear with me for five seconds," she requests before gliding the small light across and back his left eye, then right. "Good." She smiles.

"What's going on?"

Connie pulls me aside. "It is very common with a head injury to be sensitive to light and noise. The doctor is on his way to check him out. In the meantime, hold his hand to reassure him that you are here."

I go sit on one side of the bed while Abby sits on the other. She's holding his hand and softly talking to him. I take his other hand and he gives it a squeeze. My son is coming back to me. However, the joy I feel is quickly wiped away by the thought of what he has to face. Why has he been given this burden to carry?

"Dad, where am I?" His whisper is so low I can hardly make out what he's asking.

"You're in the hospital, son. Try not to talk; the doctor is on his way."

"What about Mom?"

My eyes instantly fill with unshed tears. "She's fine; she's been released. You just concentrate on getting better."

Just then, the doctor comes in and asks us to step away so he can examine Brady.

"Hey, Brady, welcome back. Can you open your eyes?"

He opens them and then Dr. Cantwell reexams Brady's eyes as well as some other things like reflexes and strength. He asks him several different questions like the year and who the president is. I hear Brady tell the doctor he is thirsty, and he wants his dad. I don't wait for the doctor to give me the okay; I'm back by Brady's side.

"Mr. Johnson, the exam I just did is called the Glasgow Coma Scale. We use it to grade the severity of a brain injury. Your son scored very well." He gives me an encouraging smile. "We will start him with some ice chips and see how he tolerates it. We will keep him on the antiseizure medication and something for the headache. Do you have any questions, Mr. Johnson?" he asks. I shake my head, unable to think of any at the moment. I'm just so happy he's going to be all right. Dr. Cantwell gives Brady his attention again. "Brady, you continue to rest. I will be back later to check in on you." With that, he leaves and nurse Connie arrives already armed with the ice chips.

"Now, don't overdo it. If you do keep this down, you might graduate to some clear broth. I'll be back before my shift is over." As she leaves, I notice it's the first time I've seen her smile. Maybe we all have something to smile about.

CHAPTER ELEVEN

Brady

I WANT TO TELL MY DAD WHAT HAPPENED BEFORE, but I don't want him to think I'm nuts. I know I saw myself sitting in the chair next to my bed. I remember every word the police said to him. I still can't figure out how that could even be possible. I look over and Dad is fast asleep in the chair. He has a tight grip on my hand. Ms. Scott is on her iPad. I wonder why she's still here. I keep thinking back to my last conversation with her and it makes me wonder which one of her eyes is glass. When I told Dad, he said to keep it to myself, but not sure how I can look her in the eye and not wonder which one. When I squeeze his hand, his head pops up.

"Dad, thirsty." I whisper.

"Hey, you're awake. I'll get you some ice chips." He gets up and Ms. Scott steps over and takes my hand.

"Welcome back, Brady."

If I keep my eyes closed, I won't get caught up in the whole "which eye is glass" thing. "Hey, Ms. Scott, have you been here all night?"

"Of course, I have; you're one of my favorite students. Can you open your eyes?"

I take a deep breath and slowly open them. I try not to stare, but I can't help it. "I still have a headache."

"Brady, you know you talk in your sleep." She has a huge smile and it's so obvious even to me that she's trying not to laugh. Now I'm nervous about what I was saying. Did I say what I did? I don't think she would be laughing about it. She leans in close and whispers in my ear. "It's my right eye." She begins to laugh, and I laugh along with her.

"I'm sorry. I was really curious after you told me. I promise I won't tell anyone."

"Thank you."

My dad is back with the ice chips and he is smiling. Something I haven't seen in a long time.

"Brady, it's so good to see you awake and laughing. I let the nurse know you're up."

Ms. Scott takes the ice chips and helps me with them. She is so kind and helpful, something I'm not used to. I want to talk to Dad about everything, but I know I need to be alone with him. I doubt I'll have a chance anytime soon. The nurse comes in and gives me the once over again before talking to dad. This is a different nurse; she doesn't talk directly to me like nurse Connie did. She's only talking to my dad; she's treating me like a child. I guess, at thirteen, I still am, but I'm also the kid who stabbed his mother after taking repeated beatings from her. He leaves and dad comes back to my bedside. "Is everything okay?" I ask.

"Yes, everything is fine. Good news, they are going to start you on liquids and soft food today. If you do good, you will be going home soon. The nurse let me know that the doctor is going to run some more tests just to be on the safe side. I promise, Brady, nothing to worry about."

"Good, because I'm really hungry. When can I talk to Danni?"

"I promised her as soon as you were able to talk you would call her." He passes me my phone. So, I wonder what Danni said to him. Sometimes it's hard for her to control her feelings. I look at the phone and notice it's Sunday, which means I've been out for three days! "Dad, do you think I can have a little privacy while I call Danni, please?"

"Sure. Abby and I will go get some coffee. Oh, and I forgot to tell you, you have a security guard right outside your door. It's for your protection."

Jesus, what else is he keeping from me?

When they are out the door, I call Danni. "Hey, I'm alive and awake."

"Oh, my God, did your dad tell you I tried to get in there yesterday?" And so it begins—secrets and lies.

"No. All he said was he promised you he would tell me to call you."

"Can I come and see you?"

"Apparently, I have security, but you can come. How did the tryouts go?"

"Oh, Brady, that was days ago. I'll tell you everything when I see you. I'll get my mom to drive me over. Do you want me to bring you anything?"

"Hell yeah! I want a strawberry shake from Shake Shack, please."

"Okay, I'm on it. See you soon!" She hangs up and now all I can think about is my shake. I'm messing around with the buttons for my bed when the nurse comes in with a food tray.

"Hello, Brady, I'm glad to see that you are up and alert. I went and got you something to eat. It's not much but I'm sure by now you're hungry."

She puts the tray down and lifts the lid.

Please tell me she's not serious with this stuff. I take my spoon and move it around. It's not oatmeal but it looks like something you can put wallpaper up with. "What is this?"

"It's Farina. I take it you've never had it before. It's kind of like grits."

I must have the deer in the headlight look because she begins to laugh. I'm glad I'm her source of amusement. "I have no clue what that stuff is. My friend is on her way with a milkshake. That's okay, right?"

"Yes, but only drink a small amount. Do you want anything from the tray?"

"You can leave the apple juice for later, thank you."

She muddles about, checking all the machines and finally finishes up as my dad comes back alone.

"Where is Ms. Scott?"

"She went home. She said she will come back tonight. Did you get in touch with Danni?"

"Yeah, she's on her way with a shake for me." He arches his eyebrow, takes a deep breath. I know what he's going to say, and I stop him before he can even start. "Don't worry; I asked the nurse, and she said okay."

He laughs and sits next to my bed. "Dad, now that we are alone, I have a few questions. Why did you lie to the police?" His eyes grow wide and he grips the side rail on the bed.

"I didn't realize you heard that. I don't want you to get into trouble. I also thought the truth would cause a stigma on your future. Besides, I feel like I'm really the one to blame."

"Why? I'm the one who stabbed her. Why are you blaming yourself?"

He puts his head down and won't look at me—why? "Son, I wasn't strong enough to do something about this sooner. It had to come to this. My son had to rescue me. How do you think that makes me feel?"

"Dad, I know what I did was wrong. I know I have to answer for it. You can't blame yourself for any of this. I could have asked for help the same way you could have. We were both too scared to do anything. I have to tell you, though, that Danni knew what was going on. She begged me to talk to her mom and get some help. I kept putting it off."

He looks up at me with wide eyes. "Why didn't you talk to her?"

"Fear, shame—pick one. I'm thirteen years old; I had no clue what the right thing to do was. So, I did nothing." I shrug.

He takes my hand and squeezes it. "Brady, I'm thirty-three and I had no clue either."

I start to laugh; I can't help it. He laughs too. Not that it's funny but it's more like a cracking point. You know, a laugh or cry moment, and I'm tired of crying. The security guard comes in and lets us know that Danni is here with her mom.

"I'll take her mom downstairs for coffee while you have some private time with Danni." He quickly leaves as Danni comes in. I've never been happier to see my best friend. Plus, the fact she has the best *ever* strawberry shake sure helps.

"Okay, Brady, spill; what the hell happened?"

"How about I enjoy this shake while you tell me what happened with the tryouts?" The shake is so thick, I have to use a spoon. She rolls her eyes and begins telling me all about it. "So, the bottom line is you made it. Knowing you the way I do, though, I'd say you are not going to join the team."

"You see, butthead, this is why we are best friends. No, I only tried out because Samantha said I wasn't girl enough to get on the team. I don't want to do cheer; I'd rather play soccer."

"Thank God. I was getting nervous that you were getting all girly on me."

"Oh, well, girly or not, don't think you're getting out of taking me to the dance."

Oh no, back to that again. "Do we really have to go, really?"

"Yes, really. Now, tell me what happened."

There is no reason to go into detail about everything since she's been watching me live with it the whole time. So, I give her the express version of that night. A night I wish I could forget.

She grabs my arm and gasps. "What will happen now?" Her face pales as she whispered so low, I could barely make out what she said.

"I have no idea. I'm sure Dad's lawyer will have it all figured out."

"Look, Brady, you can act all *it's no big deal*, but I know for a fact it is a big deal, a big deal to you. You stabbed your mother. I know it was to save your dad, but you better show everyone how sorry you are, or you could end up in a lot of more trouble than you think."

"I know you're right, but everything happened so fast. I'm still trying to wrap my mind around it all. I know for sure I won't let my dad go down for it."

"Do you think he would?"

I tell her what happened, how I heard and saw everything. "I know it sounds nuts, like I was dreaming it, but when I told my dad, he confirmed everything." I let out a sigh before I start chewing on my straw, contemplating asking her. I'm afraid of the answer, but I have to know.

"Brady, stop chewing on that damn straw and tell me what's bothering you!"

"Is it all over school . . . what happened?" I spit it out.

She rolls her eyes and takes the empty shake cup away. "There are a lot of different versions going around school. You know how school is—a drama cesspool. I can tell you that no one will be picking a fight with you anytime soon."

"Really?"

"Yeah, that is until they find something else to obsess about." Just at that moment, there's a knock on the door. My dad comes in with Danni's mom.

"Danni, I know you both have a lot to catch up on, but Brady needs his rest. I promise you can come back tomorrow." Danni gets up and squeezes my hand before turning to leave. Her mom comes up to the bed and kisses me on the cheek. That's a first for me.

"Get some rest Brady. If you need us to bring anything tomorrow, text Danni."

"I'll be right back, Brady. I'm going to walk them to the elevator."

They walk out and now I'm finally alone. I start to re-run that night like I'm streaming a movie. *I'm hiding in my closet because I couldn't find my headphones. Hiding in the closet only muffled the yelling. If she wouldn't have taken them, I wouldn't have heard the screaming. When I came out of the closet to look for the headphones again, she was calling him pathetic. Then I heard her yell that she would kill me in front of him.* I close my eyes; those words keep playing over and over again. My mother wants to kill me in front of my father for what? Spite, revenge, or does she hate me so much that she would get pleasure out of seeing me dead? I'm going to have to tell Dad what I heard. That's why I went into the kitchen that night. Right now, though, I need to rest. My head is pounding, and I want to try and forget about all of this.

CHAPTER TWELVE

Abby

THE DOCTOR HAS BEEN RUNNING A LOT OF tests, just to be on the safe side. Danni has come to visit him every day. Dane gave me the key to the house so I could get some clothes for them. At first, I felt weird going into his house without him, but I know he needs the help. I ran it by Josh, because that's what big brothers are for. He said Julie is not allowed in the house, Dane had all the locks changed, and Julie's not allowed within five hundred feet of Brady. Apparently, she is staying at a motel in town. The police are done with the house and released it back to Dane.

It's a very strange feeling walking through someone's house without them. It's almost like you are seeing the inside of their life, good or bad. I put my bag on the table by the front door and step into the kitchen. It's exactly how it was that night, or at least I would think so, since no one has been back here. There is blood splatter everywhere. My stomach does a flip and my eyes begin to water. The thought of what went down here is horrific.

I find Dane's phone charger in his office and his brief-case. I head into the master bedroom and at the bottom of the closet, I find a duffel bag. I'm trying to hurry up, since I really don't want to be here. I toss his clothes in the bag and then head into Brady's room. I freeze in my steps. Julie is sitting on the bed with a knife in her hand. She's run-ning it up and down the inside of her arm. She turns and looks at me, the tears running down her face. It's at that moment it hits me that she realizes who I am.

"You! All of this is your fault! If you would have minded your own fucking business I wouldn't be in this mess. Did you do it so you can get your claws into my husband, my son, or both?" She stops running the knife up and down her arm. She gets up and takes a step toward me. All I can think is *my gun is in my bag and I'm nowhere near it.*

"Julie, I don't want your family, I have one of my own. I'm not involved with Dane at all. I'm Brady's guidance counselor, nothing more. Why don't you put the knife down so we can talk?" I try to reason. She looks at the knife and then back to me. She's trying to intimidate me, but she has no clue what I've been through. I could never be intimidated by the likes of her.

"You have a family? Then, where are they? I know for a fact you call yourself Ms. Scott, I mean, after all, you're my son's guidance counselor, so of course I checked you out."

"If you put the knife down, we can sit, and I'll tell you all about my family," I promise.

She tilts her head to the side possibly wavering just a little. "No, I don't care about you or your family. I want my family back and you're going to help me get them. Call Dane and tell him you need him here. Get him to come here and I won't hurt you," she offers. I'm inching my way out of the room, but I don't know the layout of the house and I almost fall backwards. She grabs a fist full of my hair and pulls me back into the room. "I said to call him, now!"

"What the hell do you want me to tell him?" I'm trying to remain calm, hoping if I do, she won't become more agitated.

"You're smart; get creative."

I pull out my phone and call him. "Hey, Dane, I'm at the house. I'm packing up the stuff you asked for. I think you should come home. Nothing was cleaned up and I don't think it would be a good idea to bring Brady home until it is." I don't know how but I'm hoping he will understand I need help.

"Abby, I will get a service in to clean it, so don't worry. Besides, I have no intention of ever going back there."

I shrug my shoulders and hold my hands up in defeat. Maybe she will come close enough and I can tackle her or something.

"Put it on speaker," she demands.

"Dane, you're on speaker now." *Please, Dane, realize something is wrong, please.* She waves the knife for me to put the phone on the desk.

"Dane, I've got your girlfriend here and she's not going anywhere. Not until you come home so we can talk.

If you send the police, I'll slit her throat right on Brady's bed. How does that sound?" Her words send a chill up my spine. The memories are trying to surface, along with the urge to throw up.

"Julie, she's not my girlfriend. Please, don't hurt her. I'll do whatever you want me to."

"Oh, Dane, you always were such a pussy. Get here now!" She hangs up and I'm staring at her in disbelief. She went from sadness to evil in the bat of an eye.

"Sit in the chair and put your hands behind your back." She's blocking the doorway. I have no exit. I slowly move toward the chair and sit down. As I put my hands behind my back, I'm thinking she only has a knife. If I can make it to my bag, I can get my gun. That's when I see her profile in the mirror and notice the gun tucked in her waistband. Now I know I'm fucked. She pulls a roll of duct tape with all different emoji on it from the shelf. She tapes my hands behind my back. "Cross your ankles behind you."

I do as she says and then she tapes my legs behind me to the chair. I feel like a cow in a rodeo that's been hog tied. "Please, stop this now. If you stop this, you will still have a chance of some kind of relationship with Brady. Stop before you go too far!" She quickly duct tapes my mouth shut and runs out of the room. I hear a door slam shut. I'm starting to panic, the same panic I felt that last night with my husband. I try to calm down, but I feel the bile start to rise. *This is not that night, Abby, he's not here. He can never be here again.* I keep telling myself that over and over again. I'm drenched with sweat. Why did she leave? Where did she go? I hear the door slam again. I hear Dane yelling for me, but I can't answer.

"Abby, I'm here." He runs into Brady's room and finds me, quickly taking the duct tape off my mouth.

"Dane, she's gone. It was a ruse to get you here, away from Brady! Call the police, now!" He calls 911 while he cuts the tape off of my hands. Once they are free, we quickly do my legs. He grabs my hand and we take off running. I snatch my bag as we head out the door. "Dane, you drive, I'll call the hospital."

"I had all the locks changed; how the hell did she get in?"

"Do you have the number for the security guard?" His face turns pale and his grip on the wheel is so tight his knuckles turn white.

"Dane, snap out of it! Where is the guard's number?" He quickly hands me his phone as he rattles off his four-digit number to unlock the phone. I quickly dial the number, but it goes right to voice mail.

"Anything?"

"No, it's going to voice mail. I'm calling the hospital to see if they know where Brady is." They inform me that his chart has him listed for a CT scan, but they don't know who scheduled it.

"The hospital said he went for a test, that's probably why the guard isn't answering. "She got him! Dear God, she got him. No, No, No!"

He's pulling at the steering wheel and I fear he will pull it right off! "Are you sure?"

"What else could it be? Yes, I'm sure. He finished all his tests and the doctor said if he liked what he saw he could go home tomorrow. There was no more testing, Abby. The only thing left was physical therapy. They said after he had an assessment, then PT could be done as an outpatient."

I'm trying to push away my fears and memories that are rising to the surface. I couldn't stop what happened to my family in my past, but I have to try and help his family. I pull out my phone and begin dialing.

"Who are you calling?"

"The hospital, I'm having them lock it down!" I put the phone on speaker while I give them my name. I let them know that Brady Johnson has been kidnapped. It might even be in progress right now. I'm immediately put through to hospital security.

"Ms. Scott, we show him down for a test. When we contacted the nurse on duty, she informed us that there were no more tests scheduled. We found his security guard unconscious in the elevator. We have security standards in place that we've enacted now. The police are on their way."

"Are there security cameras in place, so we can see what happened?"

"We are pulling them now. However, we found a wheelchair in the basement. If that proves to be the one Brady Johnson was in, then we won't have any footage from there to go on. Unfortunately, there are no cameras in the basement."

At the speed Dane is driving, we will be there in fifteen minutes instead of the usual thirty-five. "Dane, it won't do Brady any good if we're in a crash on the way to the hospital." I didn't mean to come off so sharply, but my nerves are on edge.

"I know, but Abby, she's got him. How the hell did she

get him out of the hospital? The guard is unconscious! My son is with her, and she's off the rails."

There are police cars speeding past us with lights and sirens on. Dane gets behind one of them, and now we are really at a high speed. At this point, the only thing I can do is hold on tight and pray. By the time we pull up to the hospital, it is on total lockdown. Dane lets the police know who he is, and he is escorted past the police barriers to a room being used as a command center. The hospital director is waiting for us along with the detective in charge of the task force.

"Mr. Johnson, I'm detective Getty. My task force is starting a floor by floor, room by room search. I also want to put out an Amber Alert. Finding the guard unconscious is enough proof for me that he has been abducted. I will still have hospital security do a room by room search, so it can't be said we didn't follow protocol. I need a picture of Brady and anything else you can add."

Dane pulls a photo out of his wallet and looks at it for a moment, running his thumb over the photo before he passes it to detective Getty.

"She has a gun." Everyone gives me their immediate attention. "I'm Abby Scott, Brady's guidance counselor. I went to the house to get some stuff for Brady and Dane. When I went into Brady's room, Julie was sitting on the bed with a knife. I tried to get out of there, but she got to me before I could. She tied me to the chair and that's when I saw her profile in the mirror. She had a gun tucked in her waistband."

"I will let my men know but it changes nothing. I understand she is the reason he was here in the first place. Is there anything else you think I need to know?"

Dane's face pales as he fists his hands. "Yes, she threatened to kill him in front of me right before she hit him in the head with the baseball bat."

I didn't know that part, Dane never said a word. I wonder what else he's living with. Maybe in time, he will share with me. Maybe in time, I can share with him. "Is there anything we can do to help?" I ask.

"No. Please stay in this room and out of the way." He's abrupt but I understand why. The last thing he needs is us getting in the way or possibly finding her and putting her over the edge. Dane becomes very quiet as we both take a seat and wait.

CHAPTER THIRTEEN

Brady
How It Happened . . .

DAD HAD TO RUN OUT BUT DIDN'T SAY WHY, which seems odd to me. But, what do I know? My guard is texting away on his phone, not really paying much attention to anything. I pop in my earbuds and put on some music while we head out for more tests. Don't these people get tired of doing all these tests? We get into the elevator and I notice the employee puts a key in before pressing one of the buttons. I get a clearer look and I see we are not going down one floor like we did before. We are headed to something called LL. Since we are the only ones in the elevator, I'm wondering what is going on. I'm trying to get a good look at the employee in the mirror, but it distorts everything, so I can't really make out his face. I want to turn my head around to look but any sudden movement still hurts. I pull out my earbuds, tuck everything into the side of my hospital gown, and try to get my guard's attention by tugging at his jacket. "Excuse me, I've never gone this way when I went for other tests." Before my guard can answer, the employee pulls out a gun. My guard drops his phone as he tries to push the gun away from me. However, the guy gets the jump on him and hits him over the head. He drops to the floor. That's when I realize I'm in trouble, big trouble.

"There is no one here to help you. I suggest you just shut up and go along with the plan, if you do you stand a chance to get out of here alive." I'm trapped in the elevator with a nut, who has a gun that I can feel pressed to the back of my neck. The elevator finally comes to a stop, the doors open, and my mom is standing there dressed in a hospital uniform. The employee takes the key, pushes me out of the elevator and then takes off running.

"Pretty good disguise. You know, Brady, when everyone is wearing scrubs, we all look the same. I changed my hair color by putting on a wig, some glasses, and no one noticed me."

"Who was that guy? He knocked out my security guard."

"It's amazing what people will do for cash. You should be worrying about yourself and not the guard."

"Mom, where are we going?" I'm trying not to panic but my voice cracks, which brings a smile to her face. I look around, noticing all the pipes running along the ceiling and I realize I'm in another basement. The pipes make it really hot. I'm starting to sweat, which makes my bandage itch. She pushes me along without saying a word. There's an exit sign at the end of the hall. She heads that way.

"Are you afraid, Brady?"

"Mom, what do you want?" I don't want to show her fear, but I'm scared, really scared. Her words keep replaying in my head: *"I'll kill him in front of you."*

"I was afraid when you plunged a knife into my side. How do you think I felt knowing that my son, the boy I carried inside of me for nine months, stabbed me? My son, who chose his father over me, wanted me dead. Why would you choose him over me? Tell me why."

I try to get up out of the chair, but she puts a knife to my neck. I grip the sides of the chair so she can't see my hands are shaking.

"How does the cold blade feel, Brady?" She's rubbing it up and down my neck. I fight the urge to throw up or cry. Not sure which is worse.

"Mom, please stop. I'm begging you, please. I had no choice. You were beating Dad with my bat. You were going to kill him."

"Don't be so dramatic. I wasn't killing him, Brady. You, on the other hand, wanted to kill me!"

I keep looking around for a way out, but I can't find one. "You gave me no choice, Mom. I heard what you told Dad. You said you were going to kill me in front of him. You are the one who wanted me dead, and for what? To spite Dad?" I wait and listen for an answer. "Answer me, Mom. For what? How does killing me in front of my father help you? You can't answer me, because it's insane, like you are acting right now!"

"I suggest you shut your mouth. We are getting out of here." My head feels like it's going to crack, but if I take off running, chances are I can get away from her. She has a knife but I'm thinking I can beat her to the exit. After all, I'm a great short stop. I practice a lot and I can run quickly. She, on the other hand, only practices lifting her wine glass. My mind says I can do this. Unfortunately, my body says otherwise. I still have to try something. I wonder what will happen if I pull the brakes? Will it give me time to help myself or do absolutely nothing? I slowly slide my hands down the sides of the wheelchair. I'm about to do it when suddenly, she stops pushing the chair. Barely a second has gone by before I feel her pressing cold metal next to my cheek. The shape feels like a gun, and I just lost all hope of surviving.

"Brady, do not get any ideas of escaping. I have no problem using this on you, on us." That says it all. She doesn't care if she dies, so why would she care if I die? She moves the gun away from my cheek. I'm not sure if she's put it away or is just holding it as she continues pushing. I can outrun a knife but not a bullet. We get to the exit and when we get outside, the sun is blinding. My eyes finally focus. I can see that we are at the back of the hospital in a loading zone. She pushes me to a car I've never seen before, a black Nissan Versa. If I've never seen it, then chances are Dad hasn't either. Maybe it's new. She pops the trunk. When I lean in to look inside, I notice it's empty. Now I know it's not my mom's car; she usually has junk everywhere.

"This is where you get in the trunk until we get out of here."

No one is going to rescue me. "Is this your car?"

"It is now. Quit stalling and get in the car, Brady!"

I notice some people in the distance smoking. I want to scream for help. "Get in the damn car and don't think about making a scene. Those people can't help you. Now, hurry up!" she yells lowly enough to get her point across but quiet enough to not bring attention to us. I need to get better at hiding what I'm thinking. That's twice she's honed in on my thoughts.

I roll my phone up in the hospital gown while I slowly climb in and lie down. With a smile on her face, she slams the trunk shut. Thankfully, she made one really big, stupid mistake: she never took my phone away. I hear sirens but they sound like they are getting further away. When I look at my phone, I see *low battery*. Ms. Scott was supposed to go to the house and pick up my charger and some clothes. I don't want Mom to hear me talking so I decide to text Dad, he'll know what to do—I hope.

> **Me: Mom took me from the hospital. I'm in the trunk of a car I've never seen before. It's a black Nissan Versa. The battery on my phone is very low. She has a gun and a knife. She's very mad at me, Dad. I don't know what to do.**

I'm trying not to panic but it's dark. The only light is coming from my screen and if that dies, it will be pitch black in here.

> **Dane: Brady, you need to remain calm. Do you have any idea how long she's been driving? Or any noises you've heard. Like a train or church bells. Maybe how many turns she's made or if she went over railroad tracks.**

Me: No, I'm in the trunk. I didn't think to pay attention to which way the car was turning. Dad, can't you find me with your phone?

Dane: Yes, I'm turning everything over to the police now. Did she hurt you?

Me: No, but my head is pounding. Help me, Dad, please.

Dane: "I am, Brady. Put your phone on battery saving mode. That will help.

I do what he tells me, and I begin feeling my way around the trunk. There is a latch that is glowing it says pull with a picture of the trunk opening. If I pull this, will she know? How could she not, if the trunk flies open? Dad will know what to do.

Me: Dad, there is an emergency trunk release in here. Should I pull it?

Dane: The police think they found you.

Me: Dad, she's slowing down. What should I do?

Dane: Just wait. Don't pull it.

I can hear her walking around. I roll my hospital gown around the phone to keep it hidden. If I was healthy, I would pop the trunk and take off running. Gun or no gun, but I can't. My head is pounding. It's still very quiet. I'm going to open the trunk, what's the worst that could happen? I pull the lever but hold the lid, so it doesn't fly open. I lift it just enough to stick my head out. I look around as best as I can, but I don't see her. We are parked in front of a motel. I quietly lift it further and climb out. I make my way up the street to a McDonalds. I want to run but I know I can't. I stop a few times and look back to see if she's coming. I still don't see her. Dad always told me, if I were ever in trouble, to go into a business and ask them to call the police. I get inside the McDonalds and when I look out the window, I can see her coming. I run up to the counter and all eyes turn on me.

"Please, help me. I've been kidnapped. Please call the police! She's coming back for me!" I must look like a nut to these people. I'm a kid in a hospital gown with a bandaged head, begging for help. A rather large, older man comes out front and looks at me as if he knows me. I keep looking back and I finally see her coming up the block. She's looking in the store windows along the way. It's only a matter of time before she makes it to the McDonalds. "Please, she's coming, please." My voice cracks and my fear is finally showing.

"I know who you are. There has been an Amber Alert flashing on the television and on all our phones. Come in the back to my office and we will call the police. My name is Gil Dilbert, and I'm the owner. Don't be afraid. I'm a dad and I promise to protect you like I would my own kid; I won't let her near you."

He instructs the other workers to not let anyone but the police in the back. I follow him into an office. He sits me down at the desk and passes me the phone. "Call the police and tell them where you are. Call your Dad, too, and give him this address. I'm sure he's worried sick." He passes me a business card with the address on it. I try to take it, but my hands are shaking so bad!

"How about you give me the number and I'll dial for you?"

I rattle off Dad's number and when I finally hear his voice, I lose it. "Dad, she had a gun and put it on my cheek.

She ran a knife up and down my neck. Dad, she's lost her mind!"

"I'm almost there, Brady, hang on, son. I know you are scared but you're safe now."

Safe? I don't know if I'll ever be safe. Just as I hear sirens, my dad comes barreling through the door. I've never been happier to see him than I am now. "You made it, Dad."

"Of course, I did. I promised you. The EMTs are going to take you back to the hospital and I'll ride with them. Mr. uh . . .," Dad looks to the manager's name tag, "Dilbert, thank you so much for helping my son. I don't think I could ever repay you."

"I have kids of my own. I would like to think if they were ever in trouble, someone would help them."

Mr. Dilbert loads us up with food before we leave. For the first time, I realize how hungry I am. I have a French fry headed towards my mouth that's dripping with ranch dressing. That is until Dad's hand wraps around my wrist stopping me in midstream. "Brady, you haven't gotten the go ahead from the doctor to eat solid foods yet."

"Dad, after everything I've been through today, I doubt the fries are going to kill me." He lets go of my wrist and I pop it in my mouth as he rolls his eyes. When we get back to the hospital, I have a lot of questions that I'm hoping my dad will have answers for.

CHAPTER FOURTEEN

Dane

WHEN WE GET BACK TO THE HOSPITAL, DR. Cantwell is waiting to examine Brady. While the doctor is in with him, I sit down with the detective for an update on Julie. "Were you able to find her at the motel Brady ran from?" He's biting the inside of his cheek. Not sure if it's to calm his nerves or his rage. Either way, it doesn't look like he has any good news.

"No. We did a room by room search just in case and she wasn't there. When we got the video of the car outside the motel. We saw her jump back in and drive off. It's the type of area where people don't see or hear anything. The car is a rental. I need you to think; is there any place you believe she might go to hide out? She has to be somewhere. What about her friends. Is there anyone that would help her?"

"The only one I know of who is crazy enough to help

her would be Janelle. I've already run through the list of her friends that I know about and gave it to one of the officers. I've got nothing else to add. Did you find the guy who helped her and knocked out the security guard?"

"He is a hospital employee. I'm not sure yet how Julie knows him. We are still trying to find him."

"Can't the rental car company track their car?" For the first time since I've met this man, he finally cracks a smile.

"No, that's only in the movies. If it's a high-end vehicle they will have a GPS on it, but not on a little Nissan Versa. Do you have someplace safe to stay?"

"Not yet, but I'll figure something out." I want to ask him about Brady stabbing Julie, but Josh walks up.

"Getty, I hope you're not questioning my client without me being present."

"No worries, Josh, I wouldn't dream of it. I was just updating Mr. Johnson on where we stand with finding his wife. Well, I've got to get back to work. You need to find your client a safe place to stay," he tells Josh before he gets up and heads out. Josh lets out a long sigh.

"Everything okay, Josh?"

"Yeah, we got lucky today. Julie fucked up by not taking away his phone. Add Brady's street smarts to that, and like I said—we got very lucky today."

"I keep thinking about that phone. Do you think she purposefully left it with him?" He sits down next to me and narrows his eyes.

"Why? What purpose would it serve?"

"She wants me, and she probably knew that Brady would contact me. What better way to get me to come to her than kidnap my son?"

"You have a point. At this point, I wouldn't put anything past her. We need to keep Brady hidden away, since she knows he's your crutch. We also need to keep you safe. Neither of you can stay in the hospital forever. I'll tell you what, you go talk to the doctor and find out when he is releasing Brady. I'll try to find a safe house for you guys."

I get up and he follows me as I head to Brady's room. "I'll text you and let you know what the doctor said. In the meantime, I want more security on his room. Oh, and don't bring anyone from the last agency you used. I don't care what kind of excuse the guy had. As far as I'm concerned, he fucked up." He agrees and pulls out his phone while I check in with Brady's doctor.

By the time I get inside Brady's room, the doctor is just finishing up. "Mr. Johnson, why don't we step outside." At this point in time, I'm being one-hundred percent transparent with Brady, but he doesn't give me a choice to protest. "You have a very remarkable son. He is well on his way to a full recovery. I'm going to release him in the morning. He can't go back to school yet, so you might want to get in touch with his teachers about his schoolwork, so he doesn't fall behind. I have to tell you that right now, he's not happy with me. I told him no more contact sports—ever. He will stay on antiseizure medication for the rest of his life."

"Is that why you pulled me out here?"

"Yes. I wanted to give him time to digest what I told him without him feeling like I was rubbing it in."

"Baseball is his life. His dream is to play for the Yankees." My heart is breaking for my son. I want to carry his burden, but I can't.

"Mr. Johnson, you understand Brady was very lucky this time. The brain is a very complicated organ. Another blow to his head could possibly have an outcome a lot worse than what he's already experienced."

"I understand. Now I just need to make Brady understand."

"I'll be by in the morning to examine him one more time before I release him. The nurse will have all his instructions. I'll want to follow up with him in two weeks."

"Thank you." He leaves and now I have to put on a brave face before I go back into talk with Brady. When I get back into his room, Abby is sitting with him. "Hey, good news; the doctor is releasing you tomorrow."

"Did he tell you I can't play baseball—ever? Dad, what am I going to do?" He closes his eyes and leans back on his pillow. Abby gets up and kisses his forehead. His eyes fly open and she takes a quick step back almost falling into her chair.

"I'm sorry if I startled you. I think I startled myself, too. I'm going to give you and your dad some time alone. If you need anything, text me."

"It's okay, Ms. Scott."

"Brady, you can call me Ms. Scott when we are in school, otherwise, it's Abby, just Abby." She smiles and waves as she leaves. I pull the chair closer to Brady's bed. I know how devastated he is right now.

"I know how upset you are but, Brady, you're alive. If she would have made direct contact, things would be very different right now. Do you want to talk about what happened today?" I change directions. He fists his hands and the tips of his ears are turning red, which happens whenever he's upset or nervous.

"Yeah, Dad, where were you?"

"Your mother broke into the house when Abby was there. She threatened to kill her if I didn't come to the house. I thought you would be safe with the security guard, so I ran over to the house. By the time I got there, your mother was gone. I untied Abby and we realized it was a rouse to get to you. While we raced back here, Abby called the police and the hospital. The hospital was quickly put on lockdown, but we were too late. You really used your street smarts today, I'm proud of you." I beam. He finally seems to relax a little.

"Dad, what are we going to do? Where are we going to go? I don't want to go back to the house. I don't want to move away and leave my friends. But I don't want to worry every day that she's coming to get me or she's gonna beat me to death."

For Christ's sake, he's thirteen; he shouldn't have to be worrying about any of this shit.

"Josh is making arrangements for a safe place for us to live. I can't make any promises right now. I'm taking it day by day—hell—minute by minute. I need you to do the same."

"Okay. It's not like I have a choice, but at least give me a say in where we end up." He throws his hands up as if in defeat, and it makes me sad. He's lost so much. I fear before this is over, there will be a lot more pain headed our way.

"Deal. Now I have a question for you. I need to know what your mother said to you." I inquire. He rolls his eyes and pulls himself up further in the bed.

"She tried to make me feel guilty for stabbing her. I told her what I heard her say, that she was going to kill me in front of you. She went crazy after that and made me get into the trunk. I took a chance and escaped while she was in the motel. I figured a kid in a hospital gown running through the streets was bound to get someone's attention before she could get to me. I made it to the McDonalds, and you know the rest."

"It's been a long day; get some rest. I've got some phone calls to make. I'll be right outside the door." He's already closed his eyes and it's not long before he's asleep.

It's late, so when I step into the hall, the only one around is the new security guard. I call Josh but it goes right to voice mail. I let him know that Brady is being released tomorrow. I also let him know that I want an update on Julie's whereabouts, and the status of the stabbing. I hope he's found some place for us to live.

I close my eyes, taking a moment to let the events of the day sink in. When did Julie go so off the rails? When did my life get so fucked up? Why did I let it? Could I have stopped it? And what about Abby? I was shocked when she kissed Brady on the forehead . . . about as shocked as he was. What about the scars on her wrists? Am I about to let the wrong person in my son's life? If I learned nothing from all of this, it's that I have to make sure anyone I bring into our life is stable. How do I bring it up? It's really none of my business but if she is going to be around Brady then it just became my business. My head is starting to pound. I give up and go back into Brady's room for the night. Who knows, maybe I'll see things clearer in the morning.

CHAPTER FIFTEEN

Dane

I F ANYONE THINKS THEY CAN GET REST IN THE HOSPITAL, they are sadly mistaken. At least the nurse was kind enough to keep her voice down every time she entered the room. When I finally open my eyes, his bed is empty. I jump up, yelling his name and trip over my blanket, which lands me on my ass. Brady comes into view, laughing.

"Dad, I was in the bathroom. Do you know what time we can leave?"

"What the hell time is it?"

"Early, but I wanted to be ready as soon as they give us the green light."

I get up, rubbing my hip. "You could have let me know where you were going."

"Dad, let's be realistic here now; how far do you think I could get without you knowing?"

"Point taken. I'll go to the nurse's station and find out the ETA on the doctor." When I step outside, Josh is just getting off the elevator.

"Hey, Josh, Brady is being released this morning. I was just heading to the nurse's station to find out when the doctor will be here to sign off on everything. Did you find a place for us to live?"

"Yeah, I did, but first we need to talk about what Brady is looking at."

"What with his health?"

"No. He stabbed Julie, and he has to answer for that."

I take a step closer, invading his personal space. "He's not going to jail, Josh. No matter what, I won't let that happen." He takes a small step back and holds up his hand like that's going to calm me down.

"Calm down, Dane, he's not going to jail. I spoke to District Attorney Jenkins and he agrees it was self-defense. Julie actually strengthened our case when she kidnapped Brady. The only thing Jenkins insisted on is counseling for Brady. I don't see that as a problem."

"Is there any sign of her?"

"No, nothing. It's like she fell off the face of the earth. Until she's found, we need to keep Brady under constant surveillance. I don't think he's going to be happy; not even his girlfriend can know where he is. I can tell him this, but it might be better coming from you."

"What about Abby, is she safe?"

"Dane, I don't know what my sister has told you, but she has been through a hell I wouldn't wish on my worst enemy. Please, if you have any compassion at all, don't drag her into this."

"Unfortunately, she's already in this mess. Julie thinks she's my Achilles' heel, that's why she used her to get me away from the hospital. What about Danni? She's been Brady's best friend since kindergarten. How are we going to keep everyone safe?" I ask. His face pales as he walks over to one of the chairs and sinks into it. I think it's safe to say this is a lot bigger than he anticipated. Besides the fact that no one would believe me, this is part of the reason why it was so difficult to get help.

"I think we need to call in more help. Let's get you situated in the safe house. After that, I'm going to go talk to detective Getty. I'm sure he will be able to help us."

Even though he tries not to show it, his uncertainty comes across in his voice. "Dr. Cantwell is coming down the hall. Why don't you get Brady discharged and I'll bring the car around. I'm leaving the security guard with you." I head into Brady's room to gather up all his stuff while we wait for the doctor.

Julie

Brady escaped. I didn't want to hurt him, I really never wanted him at all. That's why I let him think I didn't know he had his phone. It was Dane—he's the one. He's always been the one. He always talked about his dreams of serving his country and having a big family. Well, we see how that worked out. He flunked out of the SEALS, and to top it all off, he got a vasectomy without telling me! Maybe this is my punishment for telling him I was on the pill even though I purposely stopped them. He came home a different man than the man that left. He grew distant and cold. Sex with him became his husbandly duty and nothing more. What does little Ms. Scott have that I don't? She said she's not involved with Dane but every time I turn around, she is there. She said she has a family; where are they? Is she divorced? Is that why she's goes by Ms. Scott? I have so many questions. Maybe I need to confront Ms. Scott myself and find out. *"Here's to you Ms. Scott."* I hold up my wine glass to toast her but it's empty. Empty like my life has been for the past thirteen years. Well, no time like the present to get my answers.

Abby

Josh called and said he needed to see me right away. It must be pretty important for him to show up at my job in the middle of the afternoon. When I asked him if it had to do with Brady, he grunted and hung up. There's a knock on my door that startles me out of my daydream. I see Danni through the glass and wave her in. "Hey, Danni, shouldn't you be at lunch? Is everything okay?"

"No, Ms. Scott, it's not. Brady called me and said he's not allowed to see me for a while! First of all, he's my best friend. Second of all, we were supposed to go to the dance on Friday! Now what?"

Hmm, maybe this is what Josh wanted to talk about.

"Why don't you have a seat, and we can talk about it? I'm sure it's only temporary. Besides, did you really think he would be able to go to the dance? I mean he only got out of the hospital this morning."

"I told him he wasn't getting out of it, even if he had to come in a wheelchair! Ms. Scott, that's what best friends do. But that's not the worst part. He said if the police don't find his mom, then they might have to relocate to another state."

Wow, it's like history is repeating itself. The hair on my arms stand on edge, along with the hair on the back of my neck. "Sometimes, Danni, there is no other way. It won't stop your friendship; it just might make it a little difficult until the police arrest Julie." I'm trying to read between the lines with her. She's never been one to ask for any help. She is sitting across from me, tapping her foot and chewing on her bottom lip. I get up, walk around the desk, and take a seat next to her. I look down at her foot and the bouncing has stopped. "Now, why don't you tell me what you think I can do for you."

"I want you to figure out a way I can see Brady. We've been best friends since kindergarten. We see each other every day. I don't think I can do this without him." Her bottom lip quivers and a tear rolls down her cheek. Whether real or not, in middle school, every day is a drama-filled day. I grab a tissue and pass it to her.

"Wipe those tears away and go get your lunch before the period ends. I'll try and figure something out."

"Oh, Ms. Scott, you're the best." We get up and she pulls me into a hug. That's when I notice a pizza delivery person in the doorway.

"Well, isn't this cozy." She opens the pizza box and pulls out a gun before she tosses the box across the room. She takes a step closer and takes off her hat and dark glasses. She might be able to change her looks, but I would know her voice anywhere.

"Julie, how did you get in here? Everyone has to be buzzed in; those are the rules."

Her laugh is sinister. "I'm sure you always follow the rules. I piggybacked on one of the other mothers. People now-a-days are trying to be so nice and polite. She even held the door wide open for me."

"What do you want?" I take a step forward and pull Danni behind me to shield her.

"You know exactly what I want, homewrecker. I want my husband back. He's not yours for the taking, bitch."

Dear God, this woman is delusional. "Julie, I have no idea where he is. Let Danni go so you and I can sit down and talk about this like rational adults." I slowly move Danni towards the door using myself as a shield. I will not stand by and watch another child die in front of me. She begins waving her gun around and I can feel Danni's grip on my arm get tighter.

"Danni, I don't want you. You had nothing to do with this. It's all her, your wonderful guidance counselor. I can't let you leave, though."

"I promise, Mrs. Johnson, I won't tell anyone."

"She's so quick to throw you under the bus, yet you'd jump in front of a bullet for her. You are so pathetic, Ms. Scott. Where is Dane?"

"We don't know. That's why Danni was here. Please, just let her go."

"You know what, Danni, you can go, but make sure you call your precious Brady and tell him where I am. I'm sure Dane will come running and we can all go to hell together." She smiles wickedly at her. Danni steps away from me and runs out the door. If I accomplished nothing else today, I might have saved that girl, and that means the world to me.

"See, Ms. Scott, I can be fair and reasonable. I can have compassion for someone other than me. I'm not the monster in this relationship. Although, if you ask my son, he will tell you I am." She sits down and waves for me to do the same. If I can keep her talking, then maybe she will stop waving that gun around.

"Julie, how did you get to this point? I mean, you didn't have to resort to violence. You could have divorced Dane and started your life over. Maybe find someone who you really want to be with. What is all this violence going to get you?"

"I want Dane. Oh, not the Dane you see today, I want the Dane that I first fell in love with. The Navy changed him into someone I didn't know. When he came home, he made his world all about Brady. I wanted more children, but he had a vasectomy without even telling me! I said till death do us part and I meant it."

"Do you think that maybe when he came home, he was suffering from PTSD?" I ask. She rolls her eyes and that little glimpse I was given into Julie's mind just slammed shut.

"PTSD? No, he's a big pussy and couldn't make it in the SEALS. He came home defeated, so he chose to put everything into his son and to hell with me. Well, you know what? I'm a woman with feelings and needs, and those needs aren't being met."

"So, you don't think any of this is about you, only him." I hear sirens and now the real test will be if I can get out of here alive?

"Wipe that smug look off your face, Ms. Scott; the police are not going to help you. Your only hope will be Dane. That is, if I don't kill you both. Maybe that's what I need to do, and we can all go to hell together."

She has no plan; she's flying by the seat of her pants and that's what makes my chances of getting out of here alive very slim. My office phone starts ringing, and instinct is for me to go answer it.

"Don't move; let it ring."

I freeze in midstream when she starts waving that gun around again. "Look, Julie, why don't you stop waving that gun around and let me answer the phone. Maybe it's Dane and you can work something out with him."

She stops waving the gun, begins shaking her head and repeating "No, no, no," over and over again. She gets up and closes my office door. It's an interior office, so I have no window looking out to the street. The only way to see out of the office is through the glass panels in the door. My cell phone starts ringing. I pull it out of my pocket, look at the screen then back towards Julie. "It's my brother. If I don't answer it, he won't stop calling."

"Go ahead but he's not going to be able to help you out of this. I mean, let's face it, if you would have left my husband alone, you wouldn't be in this position right now."

These are the rantings of a delusional person. The phone stops ringing but then starts again. "Should I tell him you want to talk to Dane?"

"Yes, put it on speaker. Tell him if he doesn't get Dane

on the phone, I'm going to kill you." She sits back down in the chair and points the gun at me. I have no doubt she will shoot me. I sit back down in the chair across from her and hit talk.

"Hey, Josh, you're on speaker. I'm okay but Julie is very upset and wants to talk to Dane. If you don't let her, she plans on shooting me."

"Julie, I already called Dane and he's on his way. Please, Julie, don't do anything you'll regret. I don't know if Abby told you, but I'm an attorney. I can help you."

She lets out a sinister laugh. "Help me? The only one you want to help is your sister. Call back when Dane gets here." She grabs the phone and hits end before tossing it back to me.

"My brother is a good lawyer; I know he can help you."

"What part of 'we're all going to hell together' don't you understand, Ms. Scott?"

Jesus, she has every intention of killing us all. "While we are waiting, can I ask you something?"

"Sure, why not."

"I get you want to take us all to hell, but what about Brady? What will happen to him if everyone is dead? Does he have any other family?"

"He has no one. But you know, I guess he should have thought about all of this before he decided to stab me. I carried him for nine months. I nursed him when he was sick. I helped him with his homework when he needed it. I practice baseball with him for hours, not his dad—me! What did that get me? A knife in my side. What did his dad get? All of Brady's love and attention, that's what. Me, I got the leftovers. I'm supposed to be resting but instead

I've been running all over town just to talk to Dane alone. Maybe you should be more worried about *me*." She turns to the side, lifts her shirt and shows me her bandage. It's bright red, saturated in blood.

"I'm not a doctor, but that doesn't look good. Maybe you popped a stitch or something. I have a first aid kit in my desk, do you want me to get it for you?"

"No, it doesn't matter. It's a reminder of what my son has done to me."

"You look very pale. I have water in the mini fridge, do you want some?"

"Why are you so worried about me? It's not going to help you get out of here alive."

I take a deep breath, trying to calm my racing heart. "I understand you have every intention on killing me, but just in case I survive this nightmare, I want to know that your death is not on my conscience, it's all on you."

My phone begins to ring and this time the caller ID says Dane. As I answer it, I put it on speaker. "Hi, Dane, you're on speaker." I pass the phone to Julie. "Here you go, Julie. Tell him whatever you want to tell him so we can maybe end this peacefully."

"Dane, your girlfriend is delusional! She actually thinks she's getting out of here alive."

"Julie, let her go. I'm right outside the school. I can come in and we can talk about this privately."

"Do you think I'm some sort of idiot? You and I both know that the minute I open that door, I'm dead."

"What do you want from me?"

"Why, Dane, why? What does she have that I don't?"

"How much have you had to drink already?"

117

"Enough to get up the nerve to come here. Now, answer my question."

"I can't, Julie, because there is nothing between Abby and me. She's Brady's guidance counselor, nothing more."

"I saw the way you look at her. You used to look at me like that."

So, not only has her wound opened up, she's also drunk. Great, just great. "Julie, please listen to what Dane is saying. We are not in any kind of relationship. Why won't you believe me?"

"You said you have your own family and that you didn't want mine. If that's the case, then where are they?" she screams at me, which is my trigger.

The memories and the pain that I've kept at bay are starting to come to the forefront of my mind. My heart starts pounding and the tears I've held back for so long dance along my lashes like the wind whipping the fall leaves into a dancing frenzy. I try to speak but the words don't come, only my tears start falling. Tears that used to be my answer for everything. Now they mean nothing. "Just like I thought . . . you don't have a family; you want mine. You've wanted them all along. That's why you called CPS on me. Well, that shit backfired on you."

"Julie, stop, leave her alone. She's telling you the truth. It's me you want, not her. I'm outside the school, Julie, let me in."

I hear Dane talking but it's like the world has tilted off its axis. All I hear is Rob yelling that I'm not enough, that I'll never be enough. I'm a terrible mother, and a terrible wife. I keep rubbing the scars on my wrists and rocking back and forth in my chair. "Please don't kill my baby, Rob, please don't kill my baby." I chant over and over again. It's a chant I've lived with since the day Rob snapped.

"Hey, what's wrong with you? You're supposed to be the one that helps these kids. It looks like you're the one that needs the help. Who's Rob?" Julie brings her attention to me. I try to focus on her voice, to bring myself back to the present. It's hard. All I want is to hold my baby again. To tell her we are safe. We will always be safe as long as we are together. I couldn't get my marriage right, what would make me think I could get my death right? *Focus, Abby, come on Brady needs you.* He can't end up alone. I take a deep, steadying breath and slowly exhale. I wipe away my tears and focus on Julie and the gun. She keeps poking me with it.

"Julie, Rob was my husband. He's in jail for life. This is not about me; this is about you and Dane. Now please, let's end this peacefully. Put the gun down and then you can see Dane," I plead. She hits end on the phone, and something is telling me that things are about to get a lot worse.

CHAPTER SIXTEEN

Dane

J ULIE HUNG UP ON ME AND WON'T ANSWER THE phone again. This is bad, really bad. The school was evacuated as soon as Danni called 911. Josh and I have been standing around, letting the police do their job. They are trying to have this come to a peaceful end. However, I don't see that happening. If you would have told me two weeks ago that this is where we would be at today, I would call you crazy. I never thought it would come down to this. Julie has fallen so far off the rails that she's become someone I don't know. Josh was here before the police showed up. He tried reasoning with her but that got him nowhere. After begging the police to let me try to talk her out of there, they finally let me. I don't know what happened in that room but Abby's not herself. She keeps saying '*please don't kill my baby*.'" "Detective Getty, I need to get into that room. That's the only way this is ever going to end."

"Dane, you know I can't allow that. We will wait her out."

"And if things escalate, what will you do then?"

"Whatever we have to do to get Ms. Scott out alive."

I turn to talk to Josh, but he's no longer behind me. I look around and find him talking to an officer by himself. I make my way over to him. "Hey, they are not going to let me go in."

"Yeah, it's against policy. I've got to get to my sister, though, and you need to help me."

"What happened and please don't tell me *nothing*. I'm putting my life on the line; I want to know what I'm stepping into."

"She really needs to be the one to tell you. Besides, it's because of you that her life is on the line. I will tell you that if you go around the back of the school, there is a door near the dumpsters. It will let you into the basement of the school. From there you can make your way to Abby's office. Please, whatever you do, save my sister."

"You have to promise me one thing: if anything happens to me, you and Abby will take care of Brady. I'm all that he has left." I put my hand out and he shakes it. Right now, I have to trust that a gentleman's agreement is enough.

I start to make my way around the building, but I'm immediately stopped by a police officer. He brings me back around front, but not before letting detective Getty know what I was doing.

"Dane, I can't be worrying about you, too. Stop trying to help, because you're not. We are going in. This has gone on long enough. She won't talk to the hostage negotiator and she won't talk to you."

"Let me try one more time, please." I'm not afraid to beg.

"One more time and then we go in."

I pull out my phone and try calling again. She finally answers. "Dane, I want to see you, now."

"Okay, Julie, I'll make it happen, but you need to let Abby go. She has nothing to do with any of this."

"Okay, but you have to come and get her."

"I'm on my way."

"Okay, Detective Getty, now what?" I ask. He's already barking out orders and then hands me a bullet proof vest to put on. Given her state of mind and the events of the past twenty-four-hours, I quickly put on the vest. We head into the school and now I'm standing outside Abby's office. Detective Getty is next to me, the police are behind me. Getty pulls me away from the windows in the door.

"You don't need to make yourself a target, Dane."

I tap lightly on the door before I open it and step inside. Julie is standing behind Abby with her fist in Abby's hair. Julie is pale and sweating. "Julie, I kept my bargain. I'm here now; let Abby go." They inch their way closer to me. Julie is acting like a drug addict going through withdrawal. When she gets close enough, she pushes Abby past me and aims the gun at my face. Abby rushes out of the room and I can hear Josh screaming for her. The police are still outside the door, ready to take her down, if needed.

"Julie, look at you. You're hurt. The blood is seeping through your blouse. Let me get you some help."

"What does she have that I don't? I need an answer, Dane."

"I don't have an answer because there is nothing between us."

"Why did you shut me out when you came home from the Navy?"

"I didn't shut you out. I was trying to make a good life for you and Brady. That meant long hours away from home. When I was home, I wanted to get to know my son and be a responsible father. You're the one who shut the door on our relationship." *I hope I'm getting through to her.* "That gun's got to be getting pretty heavy. Why don't you put it down and let's get your wound looked at? I'm not going anywhere, Julie." Her body begins to sway, and she drops like a sack to the floor. For a split second I thought someone shot her, but she passed out. I pull the gun out of her hand as the police rush in followed by the EMTs. When I finally get outside, Abby and Josh are gone. I head to the hospital with Detective Getty. I also call Brady to let him know this nightmare is almost over.

CHAPTER SEVENTEEN

JULIE'S WOUND DID REOPEN, AND IT WAS INFECTED.
Once her wound is healed, the doctor has recommended
a rehab for her drinking problem. First and foremost,
she has to answer for all the charges against her.

I catch up to Abby at the hospital with Josh. She was
just getting released.

"Hey, Abby, can we go someplace and talk?"

"Don't you have to be here with Julie?"

Josh is hovering like a big brother, ready to whisk her
away if needed.

"No, she is in police custody. I gave my statement,
which wasn't much since Detective Getty was there the
whole time."

"Okay, Josh, I'll be fine. I'll talk to you tonight." She
gives him a hug and he heads out, although, his scowl makes
me think he's not happy.

"There is a coffee shop across the street, why don't we go there?" I suggest. She agrees and as we enter the coffee shop, I begin to panic. What am I going to say to her? Who is Rob and what happened to the baby? Am I opening up wounds that should never be reopened? Remembering the scars on her wrists, I'm thinking this was a bad idea. We sit in a booth towards the back where it's quiet. "Abby, I want to apologize. I should have never gotten you involved in my mess."

"Dane, none of this was your fault. Julie needed help, and people cry out for help in many different ways. Not everyone is violent."

"Do you want to talk about what happened in that room?" Maybe putting the ball in her court is the better way to handle this.

"I'm sure you want some answers to what you heard. Julie was not so far off the mark. When you came into my office that first day to pick up Brady, I found myself attracted to you. However, I would never, ever get together with a married man. I pushed the attraction aside and focused my attention on Brady. Afterall, he's the one who needed it."

I try to act like someone as beautiful as her being attracted to me was no big deal, you know ... an everyday occurrence. Even though that was as far away from the truth as you could ever imagine. She takes a deep breath and fiddles with one of the empty creamers.

"I was married to a very abusive man, but you knew that already. What you don't know is it was much more than that. You know when you're in that type of relationship, it's very hard to see through the fog. Your self-esteem

125

is at an all-time low. You start to believe your abuser when he says you're useless. You're a terrible wife and mother. You're fat or you're ugly. People tell you to just leave. You know, it's very easy to say but very hard to do. Sometimes you can't find a safe way out, as you well know. When I married him, I knew he was hot-headed; he would fly off the handle at the slightest thing, but I thought I could change him. Most people in that type of relationship think they can change their abuser. Help them become a better person. Unfortunately, it never really happens. They don't change; they learn to show their partner what they need to shut them up for a while. After things cool down, they slip back into their roles. He's the abuser and she's the one trying to change him. Then the relationship gets to the point of no return. That's what happened to me." She pulls at her sleeves as if she's trying to cover her scars.

"If it's too much for you, you don't have to continue."

"Dane, I want you to know everything. I hate secrets and lies. My husband was a prominent Beverly Hills plastic surgeon. It started out small, him wanting me to have different procedures to make me into the perfect woman. Or, at least, what he thought was perfect. What he wanted was a Barbie doll that served as his eye candy when he needed it. When I told him I was pregnant, he tried to kill me. Let's face it, I was going to ruin what he was creating. That was the first time I tried to leave him. Unfortunately, I believed all his lies. I went back and for a while, things were calm. I believed him when he said he would change because I wanted to believe him. As time went on, and I didn't get my pre-pregnancy body back, he would become more and more violent. I finally decided to take my

126

daughter Tiffany and leave. I waited until I knew he would be in surgery. I took Tiffany and went to Josh's house, which was in Colorado. We were there for three months before he showed up. It didn't matter that I had an order of protection or a restraining order against him. While Josh was in court and Tiffany and I were home alone, he broke into the house. The alarm went off and the police were dispatched. Unfortunately, they didn't get there in time. He beat me so bad that I had three broken ribs and a broken jaw. Yet, I still held out hope of surviving. Then he turned to Tiffany. She was three years old and screaming through this horrible attack. He turned on her and began shaking her like a rag doll. Yelling at her to shut up. Finally, she was silent. He killed her. I did everything in my power to try and stop him. To get him off of her. That's when he turned on me again. I didn't care if it kept him off of Tiffany. I figured I could take it until the police got there. He kept punching me in the face. The beating was so bad, it left my right eye hanging out of the socket. The police showed up and he gave up without a fight. Imagine that. He only wanted to beat Tiffany and me. I was rushed to the hospital, where I begged the doctor to let me die. I wanted to be with my daughter. Josh said I coded twice that night, but I kept coming back."

The tears are rolling down her cheeks, so I pass her a napkin. I want to tell her she doesn't have to continue but deep inside of me, I think she needs to tell it all. I squeeze her hand very gently. "Abby, take all the time you need."

"It took a long time for the outside bruises to heal. The inside ones will never heal. I will always blame myself for Tiffany's death. Rob was sentenced to life in prison without parole. The day he was sentenced, I tried to kill myself. I was ready to go be with my daughter. I felt I put the monster behind bars and there was nothing left here for me." She pulls her sleeves up and shows me the scars.

I gently rub my thumb over them. "You are so brave, Abby."

"No, I'm not. If I was, I would have left him long before that night. Anyway, Josh came home and found me in time. He got me the help I needed. I decided to go back to school and get my degree for counseling. I figured if I could help the children in their formative years, then maybe I can prevent them from going down the wrong path. I moved here to Ohio and Josh followed me. He shifted his practice to help people like you and me, who couldn't see through the fog. He helps them find a way out."

"Do you ever hear from Rob?"

"No. I changed my name and moved here in the middle of nowhere. Anyway, he has no reason to contact me. I will never forgive him. I closed that part of my life forever. Do you know what you will do now?"

I wait as the waiter tops off our coffee, so we can have privacy again. "Well I have a few ideas, but I need to go over them with Brady. I'm sure, right now, he's panicking about the dance."

"You know that's why Danni was in my office. She wanted me to make sure he doesn't get out of taking her to the dance. I think there's more there than meets the eye."

"I don't even want to go there. I need to get back to Brady. I called him after everything happened but I'm sure he wants to see for himself that I'm okay. Can I drop you off someplace?"

"Sure, my car is still at the school. If you can drop me off there, that would be great."

We head out and all I can think about is telling Brady my big plan for the future.

EPILOGUE

I T'S BEEN SIX MONTHS SINCE EVERYTHING happened. Julie was convicted of kidnapping and attempted murder. No charges were brought against Brady. I was granted an uncontested divorce. Brady survived the dance. I don't know where their relationship will go but I do know that they will always be best friends. I resigned my position at work and sold my home. I purchased a smaller home in the downtown area. Abby and I talked about dating but we both realized we love our friendship and the support we give each other. I realize that just because I'm attracted to someone doesn't mean I'm supposed to take it to another level. What we did do together is open a shelter for abused men. It has a huge meeting room, which we will use for classes and group therapy sessions. There are places and organizations that can help women, but the truth is, there are very few for men or same sex partners. At first, I was nervous about making my journey public but then Brady told me to stop living in the shadow of myself. He told me to go out and share my story.

Today is the grand opening of Out of The Shadows, a shelter for all who need it. I cut the yellow ribbon and step inside. Today is an open house for the neighborhood and the press. I head into the meeting room, which is standing room only. To say I'm nervous is an understatement. I make my way to the front of the room and step up to the podium. I can feel my heart pounding in my chest. I look out over the crowd; some of them I know, others are new to me. The room becomes quiet. I take a deep breath and focus on my son. "Hello, everyone. My name is Dane Johnson, and this is the face of a victim of domestic violence." The room continues its silence. My fear and insecurity begin to surface. That's when Brady steps up to the podium.

"My name is Brady Johnson, and this is the face of a victim of domestic violence. I'm here today because my dad had the courage to take a stand. He's here to let you know you are not alone. You will never be alone as long as you are willing to take that first step. When I think of fear, I'm reminded of a poster that's hung in my English class with a famous quote *by Ralph Waldo Emerson: Do not go where the path may lead, go instead where there is no path and leave a trail.* My dad, he's leaving a trail for all who need it."

The End

Author's Note

Fear. It can be crippling. Giving into the fear can be deadly. Taking that first step is the hardest thing you will ever do but also the most important one. There are agencies that can help, but you have to reach out . . . overcome that fear. If you need help, you can call The National Domestic Violence Hotline at 1-800-799-SAFE (7233). You can also reach them at: www.domesticshelters.org

Male survivor:
malesurvivor.org/about-malesurvivor

Victims Connect:
victimconnect.org/about-us/about-our-services

Alcohol Treatment Center:
www.alcoholrehabguide.org/treatment

OTHER BOOKS

ABOUT THE AUTHOR

Theresa Sederholt was born and raised in Brooklyn New York. She is a graduate of Campbell University in North Carolina, with a degree in Criminal Justice. Theresa now calls North Carolina home, with her husband, a professional chef, and her two dogs.

Experiencing life first hand is what she does best. Believing she can do anything has put her in many crazy situations. Whether it's babysitting a pig farm or cutting the top off of a mini truck; nothing is ever out of reach. Her list is endless, A to Z.

Theresa's beliefs are pretty simple. There isn't a luggage rack on the hearse, and give a girl Nutella and espresso and she can change the world.

Theresa enjoys connecting with her fans. She can always be reached through her website at:

www.theresasederholt.com

www.ingramcontent.com/pod-product-compliance
Lightning Source LLC
Chambersburg PA
CBHW070936030426
42336CB00014BA/2696